T0028489

DUNGEONS & DRAGONS®

HOW TO BE MORE D&D

Face Your Dragons, Be More Adventurous, and Live Your Best Geeky Life

KAT KRUGER

RUNNING PRESS
PHILADELPHIA

Running Press
Hachette Book Group
1290 Avenue of the Americas, New York, NY 10104
www.runningpress.com
@Running_Press

Printed in China

First Edition: August 2022

Published by Running Press, an imprint of Perseus Books, LLC, a
subsidiary of Hachette Book Group, Inc. The Running Press name and
logo is a trademark of the Hachette Book Group.

The Hachette Speakers Bureau provides a wide range of authors
for speaking events. To find out more, go to
www.hachettespeakersbureau.com or call (866) 376-6591.

The publisher is not responsible for websites (or their content) that are
not owned by the publisher.

Print book cover and interior design by Rachel Peckman.

Library of Congress Control Number: 2021055235

ISBNs: 978-0-7624-7887-3 (hardcover), 978-0-7624-7888-0 (ebook)

RRD-S

10   9   8   7   6   5   4   3   2   1

For Chris, who gave me the keys to the dungeon

Contents

Introduction

So You Want to Be an Adventurer

Hail and well met, fellow adventurer! So, you picked up this book probably out of curiosity about what it even means to "be more D&D." After all, Dungeons & Dragons is a fantasy roleplaying game of sword and sorcery, featuring elves, dwarves, and goblins. Real life? Not so much. In the game, a lot happens at the roll of a d20 (20-sided die). When you think about it, that randomness is a big part of our everyday world. This book is about embracing that randomness and accepting a call to adventure while collaborating with others. Ultimately, it's about taking charge of your life and taking ownership of your story. Of course, you might also be wondering what exactly qualifies someone to write a book about how to "be more D&D."

Well, gather round the fire, weary traveler, as I tell the tale of how this game changed my life. I came to D&D a little later in life—the fall of 2014, to be exact—when I was an author guest at Hal-Con Sci-Fi, Fantasy & Comic Convention on the east coast of Canada. There I met an actual wizard from Wizards of the Coast, who had been invited as a gaming guest. At the convention, he taught me how to play fifth edition (5E), which had just been released. In an hour and a half, I fell in love with the game because the storytelling potential really resonated with me as an author.

Over the next year, after only one brief learn-to-play session, I started to run a home game as a Dungeon Master (DM) with the starter box set, and then I began teaching at a creative learning center for adolescents. It was then, as I saw how magical the game was among the youth there, many of whom were otherwise struggling, that I started to glimpse the full potential of the game. Of course, this was also right when my life was turned completely upside down. My marriage of sixteen years came to an end, and it felt like the proverbial rug was pulled out from under me. Except, for a while, it also kind of felt like it had transformed into a terrible rug of smothering as I navigated what it meant to start my life all over again at the age of forty.

There was, of course, a lot of crying in the first few months—a lot of feeling sorry for myself and scared for what the future held. But then I started to realize the perks of being single, despite my age. Eventually, I embraced it as an opportunity to grow and figure out "what now?" It turns out to be an important question to ask yourself when you're at a crossroads in life. In the game of D&D, we ask it all the time. There's a good deal of thought and planning that happens when characters face a major setback—let's be honest, at some gaming tables, even the little decisions are given a lot of thought. In our daily lives, we tend to accept the status quo until something happens to shake things up.

Fast-forward about nine months to the same convention where the very person who brought D&D into my life was invited back . . . and so was I. We wound up hitting it off in a different way this time, and by the end of the weekend, we decided to start seeing each other. The problem? We were on separate coasts and in separate countries. That's when I asked myself, "What if . . . ?" *What if* I invited him on an overseas Christmas trip I'd already planned out? *What if* we could bridge the gap?

To be honest, a game of D&D is kind of like asking yourself and your adventuring party, "What if . . . ?" There's a lot of back-and-forth when talking through a situation or how you want your characters to interact, and often, the pros and cons of a plan are heavily discussed and agreed upon before moving forward on it. It makes sense to take this approach in real life, too. Except, instead of getting hung up on just the negative possibilities of a situation, try to take calculated risks on positive outcomes.

So, what did I end up doing? I invited him to join me on that trip. And the moral of the story? In life, you don't need to seek out a special nonplayer character (NPC) to give you a quest or wait for something to happen to you. Instead, sometimes you simply need to embrace adventure. Of course, you aren't going to have as many opportunities if you are at home on your sofa all the time, so get out there and meet your friends at a tavern—or boba shop or gym, for that matter—and, who knows, maybe a mysterious stranger will appear.

Learning to add a bit of D&D into your life isn't about figuring out how to make a one-to-one translation to live your life more like your level 3 wizard or rolling a die every time you need to make a decision—it's much simpler than that. Instead, "being more D&D" is about how you can take the skills, traits, and sense of adventure that come from playing a game of Dungeons & Dragons and learn how to use those same skills and traits in your everyday life. Okay, and yes, this book will help you embody some of the characteristics of your favorite class—from barbarian to wizard and everything in between—and we definitely have some activities that require a little dice rolling, but the point is that you already have everything you need to "be more D&D." You only have to learn how to get in touch with it.

You are perfectly capable of setting off on an adventure, fighting your own battles, and supporting those you love on your own. How? you might ask. Well, the answer awaits you in the pages beyond . . .

PART 1

YOUR CRITICAL ROLE

1
MAKING D&D
A REALITY

You might be wondering how to bring a sense of adventure into your everyday life. While LARPing and cosplaying are both fun, it's not exactly practical to show up to your work meeting or first date dressed up like Dame Iain Ninelives, tabaxi bard and knight of the Order of the Unicorn. However, that's not to say you *can't* do it. By all means, live your best life! Everything in this book is meant as a suggestion. You are as unique an individual as any character you create for a game of Dungeons & Dragons. So go ahead and take the things that work for you in these chapters and, um, roll with it. (Sorry, there had to be at least one of those puns in here, and it's better to get it out of the way early.)

Of Monsters and Mayhem

What, might you ask, do elves and wizards have to do with living your best life? Yes, it's true you can't *fireball* your problems away because, among other things, that would be a felony, but that's not to say there aren't other ways to deal with your life in a more D&D kind of way. The core idea of this book is to embrace the essence of the game and apply it to how you approach your existence on this little blue planet. Outlook is everything, and being more D&D is simply one way of viewing the world as a place that is ripe with opportunities for adventure. After all, what is life if not a series of random encounters? The world around you is filled with challenges—quests, if you will—and all you need to do is look at things with a different mindset.

At the heart of what we're talking about are two words: *dungeons* and *dragons*. First, think of a dungeon as something that may be holding you back, whether real or imagined. Remember that year when we were all stuck at home? Do you ever feel like the walls of your office cubicle are closing in on you like some kind of trap set up by a kobold name Kafka? Or maybe others tend to fail their Perception checks when viewing how you *actually* experience and interact with the world and people around you. Are you stuck in a rut of your current identity? Are there times when you get a sense that your Charisma score is just staggeringly low because you can't seem to say or do the right thing in some of your relationships? Everyone exists with their own unique set of circumstances. Understanding our unique challenges takes a bit of introspection, and you can't just expect to become a level 20 warlock overnight.

What about the dragons? Well, who or what are the Big Bad Evil Guys (BBEGs) in your life? Is it the mustache-twirling president of your HOA who hands out fines for the tiniest bylaw infractions? Perhaps it's the family of squirrels that made a nest in your attic? Or is it . . . you? After all, sometimes we're our own worst critics. That said, you don't need to have a nemesis or mortal enemy. Sometimes a dragon can seem really small—like someone whose personality doesn't mesh well with yours. There are situations where you need to find a way to overcome your differences rather than simply walk away. Whether you're navigating dungeons or resolving conflicts with dragons, there are plenty of ways the game we love can help.

Character Creation

Before starting a D&D game, a player fills out a character sheet to help them craft things like personality and backstory, as well as keep track of important information like stats, skills, and equipment. However, in Chapter 10, you'll find a character sheet for *you*, the real-life human, to fill out as a character! Turn to page 137 to get started. You'll encounter more Character Building boxes as you progress through the book and will have more opportunities to fill out the sheet as you continue your journey of self-discovery and improvement.

The Right Skills for the Right Job

In recent years, there's been a lot of talk about the social and educational benefits of playing D&D. There's a wide array of skills you hone while rolling dice, not the least of which are problem-solving, working together, communicating effectively, self-expression, and more. So, why not try to bring even an ounce of that into your everyday life? If kids can attend D&D summer camp and learn archery skills, you can bring a sense of adventure into your life, too.

ABILITIES AND SKILLS

A lot of what a player character (PC) can do in D&D is highly dependent on six abilities. When asked by your DM to do an ability check or make a saving throw, you use these scores to determine how well your PC can do a particular task, action, or ability. These numbers are fairly random depending on how you build your character (or how nice your dice are being that day), just like in real life. Though, of course, you can learn to improve these stats by leveling up in the game or through hard work and practice in real life. So, what are these skills?

Strength is your athleticism and physical power. It's what you rely on for things like rock climbing or lifting a forty-pound box (always with your knees).

Dexterity is your physical agility. This is reflected in activities like how well you can dance or how coordinated (or clumsy) you are.

Constitution measures your stamina and endurance. A good way to measure this is to ask yourself, how much can you push yourself beyond your normal limits? This can be both in a physical sense, like when running a marathon, and in a more mental or emotional sense, like buckling down for a long study session.

Intelligence reflects your mental acuity, information recall, and analytical skills. Ask yourself, did you remember to turn the oven off? Anytime you help a friend solve a problem, remember your grocery list, or calculate the correct amount to leave for a tip are good examples of this skill.

Wisdom is your general awareness, intuition, and insight. A good way to think about this skill is as common sense or street smarts or anytime you "go with a hunch" or "just have a feeling."

Charisma is a measure of your confidence, eloquence, and leadership. Can you talk or charm your way out of a situation? Some people might think so, but this skill also manifests as being someone that people enjoy being around, speaking your mind with ease, or always being able to get people to agree to your choice in a restaurant.

CHARACTER BUILDING

Take a moment to think about the skills listed above. If there are some that instantly feel like strengths, great! You should think of these skills as a balance, so it isn't a negative if there are a few that you are unsure about or that you feel less confident about. When you are ready, turn to your character sheet on page 138.

Next, one skill at a time, use a d20 to help you determine your confidence with each skill, with 1 being the lowest rating and 20 being the highest you can assign yourself. Before writing down your answer, reflect on the number you rolled: Do you feel the number should be higher or lower? Why? Feel free to adjust your die roll as need to match what you feel is the correct number. Do this for each skill, and fill in your stats.

There are plenty of ways to embark on this quest to make D&D a reality. One way is to examine your strengths and apply some of the game concepts to how you make use of them. Of course, the task ahead of you could also be aspirational. Want to find an appropriate outlet for your barbarian rage or get all buff like a fighter? Have you always wanted to try your outdoor survival skills or navigate a new city with abandon? Maybe you just want to generally be braver in the face of adversity? As with any player character you create, whether you believe it of yourself or not, everyone has their own set of skills and abilities. You just might not realize how they fit into the life of an adventurer . . . yet. The goal here is to start viewing yourself and the world around you through a different lens so you can try to mix things up or gain new focus. Regardless of where you are right now, you can always hone your craft or gain new proficiencies.

Choose Your Own Adventure

So, how do you go about figuring out what skill sets you have to start on this adventure? It all begins with *you*—or at least your comfort zone. You, after all, are the hero of this adventure, and you should always feel you have agency over your thoughts, actions, and approach to life. You already know details about your campaign setting, who your allies and enemies are, and where all the good eats are. In all likelihood, you've even met a number of nonplayer characters (NPCs) who have helped or hindered you along the way—like the BFF who sends you cupcakes without your prompting or the fun-vampire who's always raining on your parade.

Along with the guidance offered in these chapters, sprinkled throughout this book you'll find tables, forms, and sidebars. These are all meant to help guide you through a bit of self-reflection.

CHARACTER BUILDING

Take a moment to think about your personality and background, and how that might have an impact on how you move forward with the rest of the book. Sometimes stepping out of your comfort zone is great for personal growth. Other times, you'll want to stick to your strengths. When creating a new PC in D&D, there are four characteristics that form a foundation. These are things that are integral to your personality and often inform how you behave. When considering the categories below, choose attributes that are really meaningful to you as an individual.

Personality Traits: What makes you *you*? Think of a couple of things that are interesting or fun about you, and write them down. Do you have encyclopedic knowledge of ice cream? Are you attempting to visit the top ten haunted hotels in the world? Try to come up with at least a couple of things that make you stand out, and be as specific as possible. Being a bookworm is a very broad descriptor, but noting you've read the entire catalog of Dragonlance in the span of one summer says something about your investment in this particular series.

Ideals: What motivates you? An ideal is a core value or principle that you prioritize or pursue. It's something that you hold above other pursuits. By dedicating your time and effort to an ideal, you can achieve something life changing. Take, for example, this ideal from the *Player's Handbook*: "My friends know they can rely on me, no matter what." Great! You're the rock in your friend group. Conversely, maybe don't pick "I pocket anything I see that might have some value." These are just a couple of examples of how easy it actually is to take the principles of D&D and apply them to your life while also highlighting something that isn't advisable to port over from the fantasy world. Ideals represent your values, and you know you best.

Bonds: What is your strongest connection? Your bond could be with a person, place, or even an object. It could be a teacher who believed in you or the neighborhood where you grew up. Think of someone who inspires you to be the best version of yourself or someplace or something you'd stand up and fight for—like that last slice of leftover pizza in the fridge.

Flaws: Okay, deep breaths. Flaws? Yes, we all have them. The key here isn't just to nitpick and list what you consider to be all your negative personality traits. Instead, consider this an opportunity to assess the things that might be holding you back, like fears or weaknesses. You are a whole person, warts and all. Knowing your flaws only helps to address areas of vulnerability.

Once you've taken a moment to do a little introspection, you're probably ready to dive deeper. When you are ready, turn to pages 137 through 139 and fill in your answers.

Once you've finished and you have your character sheet in hand, you're ready to apply what you know about yourself to situations you might encounter in the real world. Are you someone who thrives on social interactions? Do you love to explore? Or is fighting the good fight more in your wheelhouse? Learning about yourself and how to level up your unique skills and traits are things that will be discussed in the next chapter.

2

THREE PILLARS
OF PLAY

You navigate the world in a way that is unique to you, seeking out meaningful interactions and experiences with other people and your environment. In D&D, you do something similar by using the three pillars of play: exploration, social interaction, and combat—though, for the purposes of this book, we'll reframe the latter as conflict resolution. Your PC delves into dangerous sites to claim treasure or knowledge, connect with NPCs to alter the course of evil's path, and (of course) defeat monsters along the way. In everyday life, the experiences and situations that fall into these three pillars of play might seem mundane or insignificant, but, with the right perspective, they can be a useful way to refresh your outlook on the real world and your place within it.

On the plus side, you'll also get to add a little more excitement and adventure in your life. Who couldn't use a bit of that? With the pillars of play as a guide, you can reassess your day-to-day life and experiences to discover—much like your PC—you excel at a certain play style or the way you communicate has more impact than you imagined. First, we'll talk about what the three pillars of play look like in the real world and how you can benefit from using them, before looking at ways to choose and hone certain communication and play styles—just like you do with your PC—to bring that extra bit of fun and awareness to your everyday life. All right, let's get started!

Exploration

A major driving force both in and outside D&D continues to be exploration. It can be anything from a desire for new discoveries and interactions or the act of embarking on physical, mental, and emotional journeys to uncover the unknown. In D&D, exploration is often driven by needs and goals—either yours or your adventuring party's—and whatever quest you've set out to complete. Exploration can be anything—searching for a missing pet, breaking into a villain's mansion, or helping a town solve some problems that may or may not involve a creature in the mountains that occasionally swoops down from the sky to rain hellfire.

In your day-to-day life, exploration can take the form of important goals like eliminating or lowering your debt, getting hired for a dream job, getting a book published, and working on being the best version of yourself. Or they can be more intimate goals like learning the technique for making the perfect macarons, going for routine walks in your neighborhood, or keeping in regular touch with a friend.

Conversely, you don't always need to have a specific goal in mind to explore. Sometimes the best discoveries come when you aren't looking for them. After all, life is about the journey, not the destination, and it's always full of surprises.

Okay, so now that you have an idea of what kinds of things can count as explorations (hint: it can be basically anything), now it's time to think about how you get around in your day-to-day. For instance, are you someone who prefers using a map? It doesn't have to be a lit-

eral map—cartography as it applies
to your approach to life can mean
a lot of things—but, essentially, it
comes down to whether or not you
like having a plan that can take you
from point A to point B and beyond.

Or are you, in the absence of a map, the kind of person who prefers
to wing it? Or maybe you're directionally challenged and prefer to rely
on others to help guide you. There's no "right" way to explore—it's all
dependent on your preferences.

Next, consider the speed at which you travel through life. Are you
someone who moves at an energetic pace that enables you to squeeze
every brilliant second out of your day, or do you prefer a more comfortable pace that allows you time for reflection and opportunities to
celebrate moments throughout your day? Or . . . maybe you're trying
to find a personal middle ground that offers more flexibility so that you
can easily shift gears for greater balance. While these three speeds, and
the many variations between them, are important to understanding
how you wish to experience and explore the world, certain situations
may require you to move at a pace that's at odds with your preference.
Finding a balance between the pace of the world around you and your
personal speed is often one of life's BBEGs.

Every DM knows that the foundational elements of a great campaign are tied to goals, maps, and pace as well as knowing what works
best for each of their players. Without a set goal, there is no driving

force to keep PCs moving forward in the story. Without a plan, even just a very loose one, it is hard to guide and keep the PCs interested in achieving their goal. And without a sense of pace, PCs might feel lost or confused if they are spending a lot of time doing one thing but then quickly racing through other events or plot points with no explanation.

DM State of Mind

Even if you've never been a DM, you probably have an idea of what the role of one entails. Part of the job is to help you develop character story arcs and create meaningful encounters. These are concepts that you can bring into your real life. Later in Part 3 of the book, we'll explore the idea of being the DM of your life, but here's an example of how to apply some of these ideas to your day.

Start by taking your day and reimagining it as part of a quest that you have given to a player. Say the characters have to make their way to a mountain to defeat a dragon that's been terrorizing the area. On their way, they encounter terrifying creatures in the woods and maybe have to survive the elements. Then they get to the mountain and need to find their way past a magical door and explore the caves within where even more dangers lurk. Finally, they go head-to-head with the dragon, earning the dragon's hoard and the respect of the local inhabitants. Your goal here is to build an encounter, or a series of encounters, for your regular day.

- What are the objectives?
- What obstacles could you face?
- How much experience do you earn for completing each task?
- Who are some people you could draw on for assistance? Think of PCs as people who play an active role in achieving your goal and NPCs as people who could offer more of a support role.

Don't stop there! You can apply this type of thinking to even the most mundane tasks to make things a little more interesting. Domestic chores like laundry, vacuuming, and dishes should be a group quest when you live with other people. In Chapter 10, you'll find an encounter grid template to help you get started and to keep track of your progress.

Once you have identified these key elements about how you prefer to explore and discover the world around you, you are ready to start finding ways to add a little bit of excitement and adventure to your daily life. Whether it is deciding to learn a new skill or hobby, adding a little detour to your schedule, or taking a moment to enjoy something you love, you can find ways to discover new things about yourself and your world. Start small or go big: it's completely up to you.

Social Interaction

The world is filled with tons of interesting people! Whether you like it or not, being able to connect with people is a crucial component of life and requires at least a basic level in the communication department—sorry, hermits! Even if your Charisma stats aren't stacked, it's important to remember that communication comes in many styles and forms.

Having a better understanding of your communication style means you can more easily wield the power to build meaningful connections. When you figure out your skill level at navigating difficult conversations, you can also determine how you might respond to situations. Maybe you excel at active listening, or maybe you're quick on your feet when coming up with solutions. There are a myriad of ways to deal with conflict, and you want to lean into your strengths. Both communication style and skill level depend on your general ability to connect with those around you. Remember, even during a solo adventure, you're still going to need to speak with NPCs, sidekicks, and even villains. It's through these social interactions with friends, family, coworkers, and nemeses that you get a better understanding of the people in your life and their views on the world around you.

Of course, not all communication will be positive, and too often, when there's a miscommunication or an inability to effectively communicate wants and needs, the result is a conflict. Where a PC might fail a Charisma (Persuasion) check and wind up offending the one hag in the woods who knows how to remove a particular curse, you too might accidentally misspeak and find yourself unable to dig your way out of a situation. Sometimes conflict can't be avoided, but many times, smaller problems and issues are caused because of opposing communication styles clashing or bad communication habits. Being able to effectively communicate is important both in the real world and in the Forgotten Realms.

ROLL FOR SUPPORT

When you're faced with a conflict, think about how your PC might approach the conversation. Or you can roll a d6 for advice from a classic adventuring party to help guide you.

1. Hank, the ranger: "Don't take yourself too seriously."
2. Eric, the fighter: "Get everything in writing."
3. Diana, the bard: "Sometimes you have to agree to disagree to reach an agreement."
4. Presto, the wizard: "Listen to what is really going on."
5. Sheila, the rogue: "Take a deep breath and count to ten."
6. Bobby, the barbarian: "Let's arm-wrestle."

There are four common communication styles that are often used both in real and imaginary situations: assertive, passive, aggressive, and passive-aggressive. Of course, some situations call for certain styles of communication, while other times you might find that one style is particularly effective with certain people (or NPCs). There's also a bit of flexibility with each style, and you can sometimes combine them or alternate between them in a given situation or with a given person. The main takeaway is to understand the different communication styles available to you and how best to adjust them accordingly.

Generally speaking, the most effective and healthy way to express yourself is with **assertive** communication. This style tends to use "I" statements, such as "I feel frustrated when you are late for a meeting." Doing so owns up to feelings and behaviors without blaming the other person. This style helps to foster an environment that allows for open and respectful conversations. It requires each participant in the conversation to be honest and direct—but *not* aggressive. Even though this all seems simple enough, it's not always the easiest thing to accomplish. Any number of other things can block effective communication—not just a low roll on a Charisma check.

You may hold back and not be honest because you're afraid of hurting someone's feelings, or perhaps the power dynamic between the wizard and the paladin in your party is very skewed, or maybe you feel that you always need to be right in an argument. When you, or your PC, can't communicate in a direct, honest way, you are more likely to fall back into one of the other three communication styles.

One of these other styles is **passive** communication. That's when you're afraid to express yourself. You'd rather pretend the combat pillar of play didn't exist at all and let others take charge. Unfortunately, your failure to express thoughts and emotions often leads to miscommunication and pent-up frustration. Say the rogue in your adventuring party wants to sneak into the vampire's mansion, but you're certain it's a trap. Maybe you try to say something but stop when they insist the plan is solid. If things go wrong, you'll likely resent the rogue for getting you turned into vampire spawn. In real life, the consequences of not speaking up might not be as, um, grave, but they can be just as significant.

With an **aggressive** communication style, you tend to dominate the conversation. Coming from a place of wanting to win at all costs, you appear hostile and threatening. You issue commands and ask questions brusquely while failing to listen to others. If you have an opinion about something, you make sure you're heard. In and of itself, that's not a problem. The issue is you won't hear anyone else out. Imagine the fighter in an adventuring party barking orders at the other PCs, expecting full cooperation without input and then wondering why the cleric is on their phone subtweeting about the terrible experience they're having.

The final communication style is **passive-aggressive**. As the name suggests, it combines aspects of both passive and aggressive ones. You're passive on the outside, but aggressiveness bubbles up from inside. Imagine an idea you had was laughed at by someone. You hold on to your anger but wind up expressing it covertly by choosing not to share information when it could prevent a problem. So, the warlock you have a grudge against falls for a trap or someone at work makes an embarrassing mistake because you withheld pertinent knowledge about something.

DM State of Mind

When you can't get your message across, any number of things can go wrong in your life's adventure. How do you correct for that? By recognizing some of the phrasing that's used in everyday communication.

When something doesn't go quite the way you had hoped and someone says, "You seem upset," what's your natural first response?

A. "I'm not mad." (In reality, you're very mad and possibly plotting revenge.)

B. "This is all your fault."

C. "Yeah, I feel pretty disappointed. Can we talk about what went wrong so we can avoid this outcome in the future?"

D. "It really doesn't matter that much." (In fact, it really matters a lot.)

Confronting problems head-on is a pretty big quest on its own, but with awareness and practice, you can continue to work on those Charisma skills until you gain proficiency in them.

Answer Key: A. Passive-aggressive B. Aggressive C. Assertive D. Passive

The last three communication styles listed can further prevent effective communication between parties. It's often a vicious cycle that's hard to break in real life—but by learning more about these styles, you could try to adjust toward an assertive style. You could even practice by playing a character with a different communication style during your next campaign. If you're a passive communicator in real life, consider playing a gregarious warlock who has opinions. Just be sure you're not going overboard and causing out-of-game conflict for the sake of roleplaying.

On Your Turn

You can think of these little sidebars as side quests meant to help prompt you with thought exercises related to each chapter. Take a moment and have an honest discussion with yourself about your communication style. Okay, now take a breath and tell yourself it's okay, but that you might need to do some work to improve. Poor communication habits are hard to kick, and remember that communication is a two-way street—everyone is guilty of not always bringing their A game to the table. But if you're set on living that adventuring life and meeting new people, you're going to need to exercise your Charisma skills. That means making some adjustments to the way you communicate. Once you determine what your communication style is, try making these alterations to give yourself an advantage on your next roll. In fact, next time you need to communicate with someone, roll a d6 to try one of these adjustments.

If your style is aggressive:

1. Consider the other person's feelings.
2. Assess your body language. Clenched fists, crossed arms, and leaning in too closely are all considered signs of aggression.
3. Change your POV because conversations aren't for winning.
4. Actively listen. Be attentive, reflect on what's being said, and reserve your judgment. Check out the Noncombatant Tool Kit below for more help on this front.
5. Understand that your contribution to the conversation isn't more important than anyone else's.
6. Maintain focus without veering off into unpleasant or irrelevant topics.

If your style is passive:

1. Fake it 'til you make it. Build up your confidence in small ways. You can start by not apologizing for having an opinion or by changing your body language to be more open.

2. It's okay to say no.
3. Look for outcomes where everyone—including *you*—can succeed. Remember to advocate for yourself rather than go with the flow for the sake of not rocking the boat.
4. Try to not take things personally.
5. Don't put off hard conversations. Rip off that bandage now!
6. Roll for initiative. Or institute some kind of policy where each person gets a turn to speak.

If your style is passive-aggressive:
1. Figure out the source of your anger and stop lashing out.
2. Examine your motivation for communicating before you speak.
3. Understand you can't control how people act toward you, but you can control how you react to them.
4. Address the root of the problem head-on, but be respectful.
5. State facts clearly, and be clear about your opinions.
6. Share your perspective while acknowledging the other person's.

Identifying your communication style is just one part of the social interaction web, and it's important to remember that not only are there many variables at play but that there are also unknowns. Just like in D&D, when you're trying to have a conversation with someone, you're essentially rolling dice. So, when you're trying to flirt with someone or maybe trying to make a better impression with a coworker, remember that there are only so many things you can control.

For example, the person you're trying to woo might be having an off day, so your advances might seem annoying to them. Or you might not know that the reason your workplace nemesis is hostile toward you is because of a perceived slight on your first day in the office. You could send flowers in either case but accidently make matters worse because the florist arranges thirteen stems and oops—the recipient has triskaidekaphobia! This is all to say, life is pretty random, and even when you are able to adjust and control your end of the conversation, sometimes life just gets in the way—which is something that will be covered in Chapter 3.

CHARACTER BUILDING

Now that you've learned a little more about different communication styles, turn to page 138 to fill in the style that fits you best. Try to answer honestly, and any uncomfortable feelings you have are a good sign that you are thinking critically about yourself and how you might like to improve.

Conflict Resolution

Rolling a natural 1 comes with consequences in a game of D&D, and it does as well in your life. Combat is often the easy solution and justifiable in a fantasy setting, but when communication breakdowns happen in the real world, using physical means to resolve conflict is generally discouraged. Instead, problem-solving using words—*not swords and spells*—is the route to go. Of course, it's only natural that you're not always going to agree with the NPCs and party members in your life 100 percent of the time. Conflict can happen between anyone at any time.

For example, when a PC confronts a monster that's been terrorizing a town, it can be hard to communicate with them if they aren't sentient, which doesn't leave a lot of options besides combat. Good luck re-homing that hydra! On the other hand, if you come face-to-face with a villain who has motives and can be reasoned with, other options become available. Depending on your game, there's a chance that the bad guys you're facing are pure evil, in which case, you have the freedom to smite them to your heart's content if that's what you and the group agree to do—even when battling evil, there's communication involved!

In your everyday life, however, the people you encounter—no matter how much you dislike some of them—aren't a black hole of evil and are sentient, which means that you don't have a free pass to deal a hefty bit of damage to them. While conflicts are, unfortunately, sometimes inevitable, the way you handle that conflict is completely up to you.

So, how you approach conflict resolution in real life is dependent on you and also on the other party. Keep in mind that you can be a great communicator but still roll poorly on your Persuasion check—some people can't be reasoned with, and others make demands that maybe you can't agree to. Trying to resolve every conflict amicably is always the best thing to do, but sometimes it's okay to acknowledge that maybe it's a good idea to bring in a mediator, and there are even times when it's certainly better to just walk away. The good news is that once the conflict is resolved—or sometimes even when it isn't—the story still continues and so too does your life.

NONCOMBATANT TOOL KIT

If you thought this book was going to include ways to smash things in real life, sorry to disappoint. For that, maybe think about taking up boxing, fencing, or LARPing to help you battle those frustrations and problems away! Outside of actual dungeons and actual dragons, "combat" in your day-to-day often requires a more nuanced approach. That's where good conflict resolution skills come into play! All the same, these skills are interchangeable both in your daily life and at the gaming table. Whether it's with a friend, family member, coworker, or that morally gray NPC that you keep running into, these are skills that can help resolve conflict in a healthy, constructive way.

Problem Identification: Open communication is key in a dispute. Being able to express how you each feel about the situation as well as sticking to the facts is the best way to make sure that each party knows the other is being open and honest. It's important to focus on the real problem at hand during conversations, and not what the other person did, to avoid causing more emotional turmoil and adding another unnecessary level of drama to the current conflict. Imagine, if you will, that your adventuring party decides to split up, and you wind up getting bitten by a wererat. The problem isn't that the group went in different directions so much as you're now cursed with lycanthropy and not even the cool wolf kind.

Active Listening: Now that you've got keen rat hearing, this one should be pretty easy. When you engage in active listening, you're hearing what the other person has to say *without* interrupting. Sometimes that is going to be difficult when emotions are running high or when you're still reacting to the situation, so remember to try to be objective. Push past the sensation of rat venom coursing through your veins. It sometimes helps to ask open-ended questions to clear the conversation and ensure that each side understands what the other person thinks and how they feel. "How does someone cure lycanthropy?" is a good place to start in this example. In the real world, you can ask questions like "Can you tell me more about that?" or "What are your thoughts on that?"

Negotiation: Depending on the type of conflict or issue at hand, negotiations can be more of a direct exchange or something more fluid that takes place throughout the conversation rather than at a specific point. It's important to discuss all the options and try to look for solutions that will benefit everyone in some way. Compromising and finding a middle ground are not always going to be easy—or always mean everyone benefits equally—but it is often the best way to help resolve a conflict. Maybe it means letting the laundry pile up so you can have quality family time. However, don't feel pressured to come up with an answer right away, and never feel guilty or uncertain about bringing in an objective third party for ideas or mediation if needed. Maybe the wererat who bit you can take you to its leader if you can convince the innkeeper whose basement they're all occupying to provide cheese during happy hour.

Agreement: Obviously, the goal is to agree on an option that benefits all parties to some extent. Keep in mind that when one party wins through aggressive behavior or the other party simply gives in, you have not come to a fair agreement, and it means you'll have outcomes that don't resolve the underlying causes of the original conflict. Maybe the rat king and innkeeper come to an agreement about basement room and board in exchange for maintaining the building. That still leaves you furrier than you started. To achieve a true, balanced agreement, it is crucial to take the proper time and care to remain calm and actively listen when addressing the core problem instead of reacting at that moment, then negotiate solutions that address the needs and wants that have surfaced during the conversation. Hopefully it's not a full moon when you need to have this chat!

The Inner Life of an Adventurer

When out exploring your neighborhood, you turn the corner and discover a brand-new coffee shop. Do you go in or maybe walk past and make a mental note to come back? Say you decide to go in, then someone starts to strike up a conversation with you in line. How do you react? Do you share a funny story about your pet or just smile and nod? You go and place your order, but—since you might have been a little distracted by the conversation—there ends up being a mistake made on your order. Do you shrug it off or have it remade?

As you read through the scenario above, you probably already knew and were playing out what you would do or how you would generally act without having to think too hard about it. That's because you understand your personality and know how you interact with the world. Your life is your "campaign," and in the world of D&D, this self-awareness would be called your *play style*.

Whether you are a combative, ask-questions-later kind of person or someone who prefers to sit back and watch things unfold, or maybe someone who reacts differently depending on the situation, learning to better understand your personal play style could be helpful in a variety of ways. Depending on the way that you evaluate, respond, and react in a situation, you might resonate with specific types of communication styles, or the way you make choices might be informed by different information. Your play style ultimately is a reflection—albeit a bit of a basic one—of how you choose to view and live your life.

So, what does that mean? Well, that you tend to act and react a certain way, but don't forget that it isn't the *only* way that you live your life. You are a complex human being—and not a low-level NPC—so there are tons of different ways that you adjust your play style in a given day to match the situation, people, or environment around you.

ADVENTURER TYPES

When you set off on an adventure in D&D, you're generally going to be looking for a specific kind of experience based partly on plot or narrative of the game and partly on how you, as the PC, exist within that narrative—and this is where your adventurer type comes into play. Think of an adventurer type as an extension of your play style but with real-world applications.

Understanding different adventurer types is akin to understanding your personality type. You approach life in a way that is unique to you, but your attitude probably falls under one of these categories—or some combination of them. Once you discover your personality traits and motivations, it is easier for you to take up quests that meet your needs. You can learn a lot about yourself through a bit of introspection and looking for clues in how you behave and interact with others.

Collaborator: You prefer to work with others to achieve your goals. Building and maintaining relationships allows you to organize under a group's shared interest. Whether that's coordinating a neighborhood yard sale or starting a book club, you're in your happy place when you're working toward a common goal or building one another up in whatever group you find yourself in.

Soloist: You prefer to be a party of one. You are self-reliant and don't require much hand-holding to get things done. As a good self-manager, you're most likely able to meet goals within a time frame. It's not that you're antisocial—you know when to call for backup and have close friends—but you'd just rather get things done without interference.

Thrill-Seeker: Life is short, so you want to spend yours pursuing new and different experiences. You're not necessarily motivated by danger so much as undeterred by risks. You are driven to conquer new challenges and soak up every experience life has to offer. Your thrill can come from adrenaline-filled extreme sports, like skydiving, or an activity that pushes you to try something new, like running a marathon.

Philanthropist: Driven by empathy and concern for the welfare of others, you feel an obligation to do what is in your power to alleviate their struggles. You strive to promote the welfare of others through the donation of time, emotional energy, money, property, or services. You are mindful of the people and environment around you and always do your best to lend a hand in any situation—whether that's offering to help an elderly neighbor, being supportive of a friend when they need you, participating in volunteer work, or just doing something sweet for your partner after a long day.

Appraiser: When it comes to relationships and experiences, you view the world through the lens of a fair exchange. You tend to live by the rules of "you get what you deserve." As someone who knows the true value of things, including yourself, you often hold yourself and your relationships to high standards because you know your worth. If something or someone isn't worth your time, you have no problem walking away. While some might find you calculating or indifferent, the truth is that you are just more precious and mindful of the energy, time, and effort you spend on others—and you aren't likely to spend them on someone if the trade isn't mutual and beneficial for you.

No matter which adventurer type—or combination of types—you feel drawn to, identifying and owning how you engage with the world and the people in it allows you to better understand how and why you might make certain choices. If you can't seem to get that one friend or coworker to like you, it's possible you are competing adventurer types or have competing communication styles.

Character Building

This would be a good time to turn to page 139 and fill in your adventurer type! It might be difficult to select just one type that perfectly captures how you like to interact with the world, so feel free to select a primary and secondary type and add them to your character sheet. Think about how your adventurer type(s) might affect your outlook on your day-to-day activities, your choices, and even your relationships.

So, now that you know more about your adventurer type and the three pillars of play, you are ready to go out and tackle life's unexpected and surprising adventures, right? The topics covered here are a crucial part of D&D's framework, but they're also very useful in creating a foundation to help you navigate your day-to-day adventures. With these topics successfully unlocked, you now have the tools to further your exploration of your surroundings, add a little spice to your day, and have healthier, more positive relationships and interactions with yourself and people around you. From unknowable events to random NPC encounters and uncontrollable PC companions, sometimes it feels like the dice of life are not rolling in your favor. The good news is Chapter 3 covers what to do when you have to face random encounters and the unexpected.

3
NATURE OF
THE D20

Part of the thrill of playing D&D is the unpredictability of the dice. A lot of your successes and failures are dependent on the roll of a d20—you know, that twenty-sided die that's one of the hallmarks of the game. When you try to convince a shady NPC to divulge information about the hideout of a group of bandits, a natural 20 ensures you get the necessary details—and then some. When you get to the hideout and confront said bandits, rolling a 1 guarantees you completely whiff your attack. In the game, these are opportunities to lean into your wins and losses with a bit of fun roleplaying.

In real life, there are a lot of forces outside your control. Whether it's the weather, or other people, or really *anything* life throws at you, there are going to be times in your life when you simply can't predict an outcome. Sometimes it might feel like you rolled a 1 on your Perception check and missed out on a social cue with a new friend. When things go unexpectedly, there's often a tendency to rationalize what happens. You might think that friend is angry at you because you were late, but it was actually because you misheard her and laughed at an inappropriate time. There are also going to be a lot of times when you need to take a step back, take a deep breath, assess the situation, and then learn from it. But other times? You're just going to have to *embrace* the randomness of it. That's what this chapter is all about.

Crits and Misses

In D&D, it's completely possible that your PC can be proficient at a skill and yet still fail on account of a bad roll. Just like you can be skilled at balancing a budget but occasionally be off because of a math error. Conversely, a character with a low ability modifier could try their luck at something and pull off a truly surprising feat. Just like you can surprise yourself sometimes. That's the nature of the d20. When it comes to critical hits (a.k.a. lucky shots) and natural 1s, you wouldn't simply dust off your hands and declare your character has won, or flip a table because they somehow lost. So, why is it that we so often allow one bad outcome in life to affect us so negatively? Unless your character fails their death saves, one event isn't the end of the world for them. And it doesn't have to be for you either.

ON YOUR TURN

In a Dungeon Master's tool kit, there's an unwritten rule of thumb known as using "Yes, and . . ." This concept is also seen in improv comedy and asks participants to build on an idea instead of turn it down. When playing D&D, this method applies to the shared storytelling experience. Although a DM is the arbiter of rules, allowing players agency over their characters' lives dictates a bit of back-and-forth. It also allows for a lot of fun surprises.

"Yes, and . . ." is a powerful tool if used properly in real life as well. The applications in real life can mean that, when you're trying to connect with someone, you don't bring preconceived ideas and assumptions to the table. You listen first, then add your own ideas. You can brainstorm, collaborate, and resolve conflict more freely with this concept in mind.

However, it's important to remember that when applying this concept to real-life situations, there's a huge caveat: this is *your* real life. Regardless of intention or potential positives, it's very important to respect your boundaries and that of others. "Yes, and . . ." doesn't mean being agreeable all the time, rather it's the acceptance of other ideas without judgment. You can (and should) reject any ideas that are hateful or harmful. Boundaries protect you and help maintain your values.

With that all in mind, there are plenty of ways to have fun with this concept. Try it out! Below are three exercises, and the only rule is that the "adventuring party" you recruit for the activity must use the "Yes, and . . ." principle. Save any applicable editing and refining of ideas for later. The goal is to unlock the possibilities when everyone is supported equally.

1. Plan an outing with someone by building on each other's ideas. You want to go to the beach, and your friend suggests learning how to surf.
2. Brainstorm on a project with someone whether it's a work task, home improvement project, or creative endeavor without shooting down ideas. Let's say you're renovating the kitchen and your partner mentions wanting a counter for barstools but there's not enough room with the current configuration. If it's in budget, you can "Yes, and . . ." a pesky wall away.
3. Have a Yes Day with friends or family. This is pretty straightforward, since the day embraces saying yes to just about anything.

Embracing the randomness of life becomes a lot easier when you realize there are similarities between D&D and your everyday experience. Flexibility in outlook and adaptive thinking can go a long way both in and out of the game. When life hands you 1s, just roll with it. Eventually, a 20 will turn up.

Roll with It

Life doesn't always go as planned. From little setbacks (like your food order missing a key ingredient) to bigger, more troublesome situations (like your living space being flooded), similar to your latest campaign, there's a certain amount of randomness that occurs in the real world. The only difference is that in D&D you have someone (*cough*, the DM) or something (*cough*, bad dice) to direct your ire at. When things go wrong in your day-to-day life, it's sometimes much harder to accept or address your feelings because there isn't always an easy place where you can direct them. Of course, life's little random things aren't always bad. In fact, windfalls such as a coworker dropping off your favorite warm beverage at your desk, pulling up to a parking meter that has time left on it, or inheriting money from a long-lost relative are also chance occurrences.

You may try to explain *why* these things happen. It's a natural human reaction, particularly in situations where things haven't gone your way. Since there isn't always an explanation for why these things happen, most people try to create a narrative or find ways to rationalize outcomes, whereas in your game of D&D, characters tend to face their problems head-on. Here are some everyday examples of how we process interactions:

- **Time Stop:** A conversation doesn't go the way you'd hoped, and you relive the moment in your head, playing out how things might have gone if you'd said something else.

- **Meta-Gaming:** You're nervous about an upcoming event, so you plan for every possible outcome in your head.
- **Insight Check:** You try to stay one step ahead by figuring out a person's motives for doing something—without asking them up front.

When you do this, you're actively changing the narrative and weaving a story that allows you to come to terms with, understand, or accept an outcome. In D&D, your character probably asks a lot of questions or at least tries to follow up with leads or figure out why something didn't go as planned. Shrugging something off as "fate" or "bad luck" doesn't help solve the *why*. When you rationalize why something happened, you're creating a *manufactured* truth. Unless you can ask the source directly, you're not going to know what a person's motivation is for doing something. So, good luck getting in touch with Silvanus, god of nature, about that flood situation.

Instead of rationalizing *why* the wheel of fortune has landed on weal or woe, use that energy to think and then act or to embrace a situation. Accepting the randomness that has come your way might open up opportunities. Say you return the gesture with that fairy god barista who delivered the coffee to your desk the other day. Maybe it will be the starting point for a great friendship or even romance. Or follow up with a hiring manager on a job rejection and ask to be considered for future opportunities that may be a better fit.

ROLL FOR INITIATIVE

Reacting to what life throws at you takes practice. Next time you get together with people who are close to you, whether it's family or your D&D group, try working out a question or issue by using the round-robin method. Roll for initiative at a table and use turn order for participants. The first person responds with a single thought or reaction, either out loud or on a piece of paper. Everyone else waits their turn. The next person in the turn order contributes an additional point, idea, or thought. And so on. Whether it's a plan for entering a dragon's lair or what to do about the household chores, you can have a bit of fun while also problem-solving.

And what happens if, while embracing the chaos of life, you mess up along the way? Those moments when you grab the situation by the horns and make that bold choice, but instead of landing that critical hit or finding that hidden treasure, you end up taking damage and having to face that mimic after all. It's all bound to happen to us sometime, but the positive thing to take away is that you tried. Maybe take it as a chance to lighten up and laugh at yourself. Nobody is perfect—life's dice ensure it. So, when you dig deeper, make connections, give yourself time to think before acting, and ask important questions, you're learning to be flexible and thoughtful, and by following the lead of the random things that happen in your life, sometimes truly good and exciting things can happen.

ROLL FOR SUPPORT

Need some inspiration for dealing with random life events? Roll a d6 to see how our classic adventuring party might react to plans not going as intended.

1. Hank, the ranger: "You can't anticipate everything, but maybe you can learn something from the unanticipated."
2. Eric, the fighter: "Wishing this away isn't going to help. I've tried that already. You're going to have to stick it out and hope for the best."
3. Diana, the bard: "Sometimes you just need to go with the flow."
4. Presto, the wizard: "Many mysteries show up to challenge and push your limits."
5. Sheila, the rogue: "Life is full of surprises. Isn't it great?"
6. Bobby, the barbarian: "Smash through whatever obstacles life throws at you."

Randomize Your Life

One way to embrace the things that life rolls your way is through random acts of kindness. After all, what's more heroic than doing something for the greater good? It's these small, consistent acts of kindness that can have a ripple effect for spreading compassion and can add in a bit of positive randomness into someone's life—including yours! Below you'll find some d20 tables that are prompts for random acts of kindness that you can incorporate into your life. These are meant as inspiration, so feel free to skip or find your own unique spin on these acts of kindness by filling in the blank table provided below.

Integrate random acts of kindness into your life with ideas you generate, too. If you're introverted or intimidated by talking to strangers, you can always try this out on people you know. Eventually, the acts of kindness will spread further out from you, and before you know it, the kindness will reach strangers. The key is to not overthink your random act of kindness! Even the simplest things can make a difference.

RANDOM ACTS OF KINDNESS TABLE

d20	Random Act
1	Leave positive comments for people on social media.
2	Leave a basket of snacks and bottled or boxed water by your front door at home and at work for delivery drivers.
3	Fill a bag with snacks, water, and hygiene products and give to an unhoused person.
4	Paint kind words on rocks and leave them at a park.
5	Make bookmarks with notes of encouragement to leave in random books at the library.
6	Have flowers or treats delivered to the nurses' station at your local hospital.
7	Donate any extra canned food to a food bank or community fridge/pantry.
8	Leave unused coupons next to corresponding products in the grocery store.
9	Write an encouraging note with sidewalk chalk outside to brighten the day of people who see it.
10	Start a piggy bank for a cause and donate all your loose change at the end of the year.
11	Share some online love by writing a review for a business or author you admire.
12	Sign up for a shift at your local soup kitchen.
13	Visit a nursing home and read books to or play board games with residents.
14	Start a Little Free Library in your neighborhood.
15	Donate new toys to a children's charity or shelter.
16	Buy school supplies for a teacher.
17	Send cards to uplift the spirits of hospitalized sick kids through national or international groups.
18	Sign up as a storyteller at your local library.
19	Share a positive news story online.
20	Have a cleanup party at a beach or park.

PERSONAL RANDOM ACTS OF KINDNESS TABLE

d20	Random Act
1	Do something you love: draw, read, exercise, and so on. Whatever it is, do it for you.
2	Counter any negative thoughts, self-doubt, or judgment with "I'm enough."
3	Go on a nature walk—and bring a loved one or pet!
4	Practice a moment of self-reflection today.
5	Get up early to appreciate the sunrise.
6	Join a group that shares your interests.
7	Write a letter to yourself to read at a future date.
8	Check in with a friend or family member you haven't heard from in a while to make sure they're doing well.
9	Cook a nutritious meal for yourself.
10	Plan to do one thing outside your comfort zone each day this week.
11	Forgive someone with whom you've been struggling for a while—if not to be kind to them, then to be kind to yourself.
12	Send a handwritten letter to someone who's made a difference in your life.
13	Treat a good friend to a movie either at a theater or an online watch party.
14	Write a gratitude list in the morning and again in the evening.
15	Organize a picnic with friends, family, or yourself.
16	Share a friend's blog, business website, or art on social media.
17	Plan your perfect day, and then go out and live it.
18	Write a letter to your younger self and forgive past regrets.
19	Be an accountability buddy for a friend who needs it.
20	Send a silly card to brighten someone's day.

RANDOM ACTS OF KINDNESS TABLE (BLANK)

d20	Random Act
1	
2	
3	
4	
5	
6	
7	
8	
9	
10	
11	
12	
13	
14	
15	
16	
17	
18	
19	
20	

PART 2

CHARACTER BUILDING

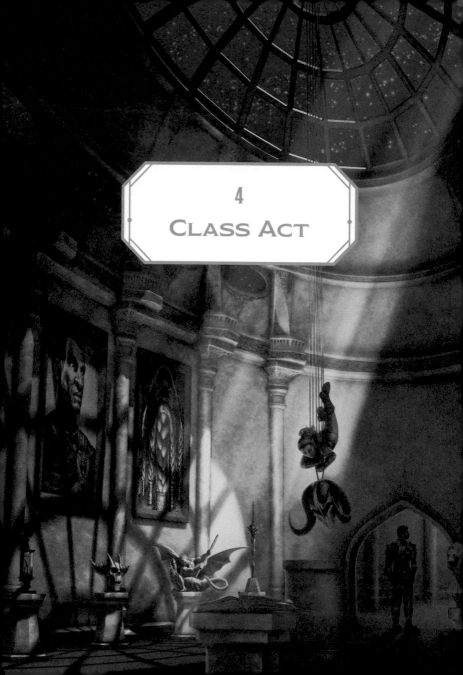

4
CLASS ACT

More than a job, a class is an adventurer's calling. In D&D, a class helps the PC establish their place in the world and often will shape their views of the world and the people in it in some way. A warlock is defined by their pact with an otherworldly patron, while a ranger is an independent explorer of the natural world. When applying a class to your daily life, it becomes more about your mindset (how you approach challenges) and your role (in relation to the world around you) rather than a hard-and-fast calling. Take, for example, the rogue class. In the *Player's Handbook*, this type of character is known for making a shady living through trickery and deception. However, that's not exactly ideal outside a fantasy setting! Say no to creative accounting, highway robbery, and IP theft. Instead, the idea is to look at the class through a more everyday lens, so a rogue-like approach to challenges means you view problems from all angles or might be open to borrowing or building on someone's idea or other more creative alternatives. Your role in relation to the world around you is that of someone who is meticulous at planning and can think outside the box because you don't necessarily conform to norms.

There are twelve basic classes in D&D—some you might know, and others might be new to you. They are barbarian, bard, cleric, druid, fighter, monk, paladin, ranger, rogue, sorcerer, warlock, and wizard. As you explore this section of the book, you'll find information about each class, some of their main features, and how you can use these skills, attitudes, and traits of a particular class to benefit you in different areas of your life like your day-to-day, professional, and romantic lives.

Perhaps you are already an experienced adventurer, and you know what class you enjoy playing or even what class best captures who you are in all your glory. Or maybe there's a class you tend to play or resonate with, but you really aspire to be a different one. Or maybe this is all new to you and you just wish there were a quiz you could take to help you figure out what might work for you. Well, look no further.

CLASS QUIZ

What better way to figure out your class than by taking a fun quiz? The questions below are meant to cover some of the basic personality traits, views, and attitudes of the twelve classes. Like everything else in this book, this quiz is similar to the Deck of Many Things (a deck of cards in D&D that has magical effects). It's meant to be a guide and possibly a clever talking point that will dazzle someone at a dinner party. So, if you know in your *heart of hearts* that you're a charismatic bard, by all means, go ahead and skip ahead or just ignore the results if they don't match your expectations. Who says that you can't be a fighter who is also a history buff like a wizard? That's right, no one. So, go on and live your most fabulous multiclass life. Are you ready to find out your class?

1. When faced with a problem, you usually
   a. Smash things
   b. Meditate
   c. Talk things out
   d. Read up on possible solutions

2. Someone keeps stealing your lunch from the office fridge. You
   a. Make two lunches going forward
   b. Post an angry note on the fridge
   c. Hold a meeting about it
   d. Stake out the kitchen until you catch the culprit

3. How would your friends describe your personality?
   a. Empathetic
   b. Resourceful
   c. Gifted
   d. Ambitious

continued on next page

4. You win the lottery. What do you do with your earnings?

    a. Build an enormous home library

    b. Buy a cottage

    c. Donate most to charity or share it with friends

    d. Buy a private island and throw a party for your closest friends

5. You're at your best when

    a. Training and achieving mastery

    b. Surrounded by nature

    c. Tending to your soul

    d. Engaged with innovative endeavors

6. It's been a rough day. How do you unwind?

    a. Go for a run

    b. Hang out with friends

    c. Yoga

    d. Read a book

7. Which person are you in your friend group?

    a. The parent

    b. The smart one

    c. The mischievous one

    d. The athletic one

Answer key: Check the boxes in the grid below with your answers, then tally the results. The class with the most checkmarks is your class. If you happen to tie, you've multiclassed!

	1	2	3	4	5	6	7
Barbarian	☐	☐	☐	☐	☐	☐	☐
Bard	☐	☐	☐	☐	☐	☐	☐
Cleric	☐	☐	☐	☐	☐	☐	☐
Druid	☐	☐	☐	☐	☐	☐	☐
Fighter	☐	☐	☐	☐	☐	☐	☐
Monk	☐	☐	☐	☐	☐	☐	☐
Paladin	☐	☐	☐	☐	☐	☐	☐
Ranger	☐	☐	☐	☐	☐	☐	☐
Rogue	☐	☐	☐	☐	☐	☐	☐
Sorcerer	☐	☐	☐	☐	☐	☐	☐
Warlock	☐	☐	☐	☐	☐	☐	☐
Wizard	☐	☐	☐	☐	☐	☐	☐

1. a. Barbarian, Fighter, Sorcerer / b. Cleric, Druid, Monk / c. Bard, Paladin, Ranger, Rogue / d. Warlock, Wizard

2. a. Druid, Monk, Wizard / b. Barbarian, Fighter, Sorcerer / c. Bard, Cleric, Paladin / d. Ranger, Rogue, Warlock

3. a. Cleric, Monk, Paladin / Druid, Ranger, Rogue / c. Bard, Sorcerer, Wizard / d. Barbarian, Fighter, Warlock

4. a. Bard, Wizard / b. Barbarian, Druid, Ranger / c. Cleric, Monk, Paladin / d. Fighter, Rogue, Sorcerer, Warlock

5. a. Fighter, Rogue, Warlock / b. Druid, Ranger, Barbarian / c. Cleric, Monk, Paladin / d. Bard, Sorcerer, Wizard

6. a. Barbarian, Fighter, Ranger / b. Bard, Rogue, Sorcerer / c. Druid, Monk, Paladin / d. Warlock, Wizard

7. a. Paladin, Ranger, Sorcerer / b. Cleric, Druid, Warlock, Wizard / c. Bard, Rogue / d. Barbarian, Monk, Fighter

The various classes of D&D define the game, and by choosing one, you can better define your role in life. They are each based on a character archetype and can help you see the bigger picture. Each class represents a mixture of characteristics, and what you bring to the class is what makes it unique.

Class Summaries

Along with having different strengths, weaknesses, and identities, each class has its own variety of special traits. On account of special training, a PC relies on a primary ability or abilities from among the following (described in detail in Chapter 1): Strength, Dexterity, Constitution, Intelligence, Wisdom, and Charisma. A bard, for example, is highly skilled in Charisma and generally relies on charm and wit in most situations rather than brute force. In the real world, much the same is true. You likely lean on abilities that you're good at and avoid the ones you're not so skilled at. It's human nature to want to do well or see yourself succeed. Outside a fantasy setting, a bard is someone who can talk their way out of trouble or into an exclusive party.

Below is a table that summarizes the twelve classes in a way that can be more applicable to your life. Be sure to add your primary ability and traits to your character sheet, which you'll find in Chapter 10 on page 140.

Class	Description	Primary Ability	Traits
Barbarian	Bold and ambitious, you dive headfirst into even the most challenging situations.	Strength	You get angry, then forget why Will do anything on a dare Hate to be constrained
Bard	You are deeply intuitive and a jack of all trades who can fill many roles.	Charisma	Can't remember if you dreamed it or if it actually happened Excessively romantic Vacillate between pride in your work and imposter syndrome
Cleric	You are a humanitarian-focused, visionary, and progressive soul interested in making the world a much better place.	Wisdom	Devoted to those you choose More in love with humanity than individuals You think about mortality and morality . . . a lot
Druid	Your love of nature is only matched by your resourcefulness.	Wisdom	Wanderlust is your middle name Unrelenting thirst for knowledge Super adaptable
Fighter	You are a determined and dependable leader who prefers to face problems head-on.	Strength or Dexterity	Carve your own path in life Unignorable You probably look cool in a leather jacket
Monk	You strive to find balance between your physical and spiritual being.	Dexterity and Wisdom	You insist on quality over quantity Tend to ponder deeply on all matters You know how to unwind and chill

Class	Description	Primary Ability	Traits
Paladin	Your strength is in your convictions and your willingness to do anything for the greater good.	Strength and Charisma	Take on other people's problems You can forgive, but you'll never forget Ride or die
Ranger	You are an independent spirit who embraces going off the beaten path.	Dexterity and Wisdom	Excellent situational awareness See the forest for the trees Know the value of home-field advantage
Rogue	Your precision and planning set you apart from others, but so too does your sense of right and wrong.	Dexterity	Can fit in anyplace, anytime, with anyone You always have a trick up your sleeve Can see every angle to a situation, problem, or discussion, which is both a blessing and a curse
Sorcerer	You are gifted with innate talents, which often put you at the center of attention.	Charisma	Protective of your squad You always stand out in a crowd Go big or go home
Warlock	You are a diligent negotiator who is a master of self-control.	Charisma	Hard work beats talent Driven to do your utmost best You know the value of having a good mentor
Wizard	Your industrious dedication to practical knowledge makes you a reliable font of information.	Intelligence	Have books, will travel Detail-oriented, sometimes to a fault Hardest worker in the room

Class Distinctions

In D&D, class features determine proficiencies in certain skills or abilities and act as ways for PCs to grow and differentiate themselves from others in their class. It goes without saying that there are going to be some alterations when trying to apply these concepts to real life because, unfortunately, you can't be a literal wizard with literal spellcasting abilities. Remember what was discussed about the illegalities of casting the *fireball* spell in an earlier chapter. So, what does this mean? Well, for spellcaster classes, this means more of an emphasis on knowledge and how you use it. Likewise, it's highly discouraged to enter a barbarian rage and smash everything in sight. While physical strength can be a goal, you'll want to channel it in ways that are more compatible with the real world, so take up activities or jobs that allow you to exercise that strength.

Need help figuring out what class to choose? "Dear Tasha" is our advice column where one of the greatest spellcasters in the multiverse stops time itself to respond to questions about livening up your life adventures.

DEAR TASHA,

I play a tough-as-nails barbarian in my regular D&D game, but my day job is in IT. How do I know what class to pick in my everyday life?

—Conan the Confused

You're already off to a good start by coming to me for advice, you dear, sweet, lucky reader. It seems you've found yourself polymorphed into a human, and you want to add a bit of excitement into your life. I certainly don't blame you! Take it from someone who's gone by many names: you needn't let expectations get in your way. First off, your job does not necessarily define who you are. I've been an "it girl" myself, and let me tell you, there are days when I'd love to just unleash my inner angst and just let out a primal, world-shattering scream! But a witch has her priorities.

Who's to say you're not a barbarian at your core? Are you passionate about—*checks notes*—information and technology? Or perhaps you have some other interests? Do you act first, think later? Perhaps you follow the path of Rage Against the Machine? You know you best, and when it comes to choosing a class, it's not for me to decide. I'm not your mom, after all.

—Tasha

Barbarian

This class is defined by passion. You are a courageous, determined, and competitive individual. In D&D, barbarians are fueled by their fury, entering a rage to tap into a deeper well of ferocious strength. While it is a great asset when dealing with countless foes brandishing weapons at you, this is a class that can quickly drain a PC, leaving them exhausted. In real life, you want to direct your deep passion for things in more positive ways that maybe don't leave you needing a long nap. Every barbarian chooses a path that shapes their rage. You can think of it in terms of figuring out what drives your passion. Channel your reservoir of emotions into your interests.

Reckless Attack: It means you tend to act first, think later. Throwing caution to the wind can sometimes land you in hot water. In game terms, *reckless attack* gives a barbarian advantage on physical attacks, but it comes at the cost of giving enemies advantage on attacks against you until your next turn. The real-world implications of reckless actions are pretty wide-ranging. While there are certainly a lot of positives that can come from jumping into something without overthinking, like standing up for someone who needs help, maybe just an ounce of forethought from time to time wouldn't kill you?

Bard

Bards are all about music and magic—there's plenty of magic in the real world but maybe without as many spell components. You are a master of the talents you choose to hone, and you thrive when you're creating. Bards belong to colleges in D&D, and in the real world, you probably belong to a kind of creative collective for a sense of community. With a deep well of empathy and interest in human nature, coupled with creativity and imagination, you are drawn toward the arts. However, your ability to imagine fantastical stories sometimes blurs the line with reality, which makes you a bit of a hopeless romantic at times. Remember to take your head out of the clouds every once in a while.

Bardic Inspiration: You just "get" other people. With your ability to figure out what makes others tick, you've got a knack for knowing what to say or do to inspire those around you. Let's face it: in the real world, a lot of bards are introverts. That high Charisma score? Maybe it's your quirky, awkward self. In lieu of a rousing performance, your inspirational recital could just as easily be other types of things you create and how others engage with them.

Cleric

Both a healer and a fighter, a cleric often uses those skills and strengths to serve a higher calling. In the real world, this is seen in the strength of your convictions rather than spiritual devotion. Belief that there's more to the world than what can be seen with the naked eye doesn't have to be tied to a "divine domain" or organized religion. It could be a strong personal belief that guides you in your life. Regardless, you're someone who, once you make your mind up about something, won't compromise. Sometimes that means you have to stand on your own—alone.

Healing Word: You care deeply about what happens around (and within) you. With a sense of fairness combined with lofty idealism, your deeds tend to have real impact. Whether it's activism, charity, or other work, you act in a way that is restorative.

Druid

Druids revere nature above all else. To you, you were put on this earth to preserve the delicate ecological balance that exists between the environment and the modern world. Perhaps you practice druidry, but it's more likely that you lead a more granola lifestyle than your peers. In D&D, a PC of this class identifies with a druid circle. Think of it as a group of kindred souls whether it's other Scout troop leaders, members of a community garden, or your workplace green committee. You are all about keeping the balance and harmony of the world around you, but maybe you can ease up on occasion and allow some things to be less than perfect.

Wild Shape: You may wish it were possible to take the form of whatever animal tickles your fancy at the moment, but therianthropy is not an option in real life. Instead, consider this: What animal do you vibe with? Are you a clever fox, an introverted panda, a transformative butterfly? Embrace your inner beast and use that energy in your life to work toward your goals.

Fighter

Fighters represent one of the most diverse classes who know the basics of all combat styles. As a fighter, you're a well-rounded specialist. You treat daily life like a mission, focused and ready to take on roles and jobs that many others would run away from. You're also resolutely protective and loyal to those you care for. When it comes to your martial archetype, you have a choice in your fighting style. Are you skilled in debate? How do you work your strengths or advantages to get what you want? While you're flexing, just remember that persistence can become a problem when it gets to be obsessive.

Protection: If someone is going to come at you or yours . . . they'd better not miss. In D&D, a fighter equipped with a shield can react to help out a nearby ally who's being attacked. In the real world, your shield is a powerful tool that you use to help others. Is it your privilege that you use to lift up the marginalized? Or is it that you're the reliable friend who's always there in times of need? Whatever it is, wield your shield fearlessly.

Monk

As a monk, you strive to understand yourself by growing and figuring out your personal strengths and weaknesses to push yourself to your limits. Your inner strength and discipline are driven by a desire to achieve healthy self-awareness and a meaningful existence. You have almost endless reserves of tenacity, patience, and resilience. In D&D, this class follows the traditions and structures of a monastic lifestyle, but in the real world, you are likely to have various personal traditions, rituals, and habits as a means of both organization and self-care. A deep thinker, you should be careful to ensure that your eternal deliberation on matters doesn't mean completely zoning out, lest you frustrate those around you.

Deflect Missiles: A monk PC uses a quick reaction to deflect or catch a missile and can even make an attack with the same missile! Your self-control allows you to approach situations with calm. In a disagreement, you don't take things personally. Words are like water off a duck's back. Instead, you persevere with patience, knowing you can always come back to use someone's own words against them.

Paladin

A paladin vows to strike down evil and stand with good. Yours is not necessarily a religious undertaking (though it can be) so much as a commitment to right wrongs. Different paladins focus on different aspects when it comes to upholding justice, but all are bound by an oath. What is it in your life that you sense is your calling? It probably has something to do with fighting for what you believe is right. Although you may not like conflict, you are quick to come to the aid of others. In your eagerness to uphold all these values, don't forget to take care of yourself also. After all, you can't tamp down the forces of evil when you're hangry.

Divine Smite: In D&D, a paladin can inflict extra radiant damage. Your intense convictions in real life can have a similar effect. You live your truth without apology, and that will either turn away those who don't share your beliefs or spread to those who are open to hearing you out.

Ranger

Rangers embrace adventure off the beaten path. You enjoy the great outdoors and prefer your independence from others. In D&D, rangers are deadly hunters who track their "favored enemies" in the wild. In the mundane world, this may be true, but you're more likely someone who can hunt down that perfect campsite and kill some s'mores. All the same, you're used to life that's removed from creature comforts—and other people. While there's nothing wrong with enjoying life solo, or with a furry companion, there's also nothing wrong with inviting others to join your party occasionally.

Hunter's Mark: When you set your sights on something, you are undeterred from achieving your goal. Your sharp focus gives you advantage, and once you complete a task successfully, you set your sights on the next thing. And if you fail? No worries, you're the kind of person who has a plan B. And C. And D . . .

Rogue

Rogues devote efforts to a mastery of skill and precision. You prioritize cunning over brute strength and are more likely to make a precise and meaningful strike than a barrage. Pick your battles, indeed. Why put yourself in danger when you can skirt around it—and any pesky rules while you're at it. You aren't afraid to take your own path, even if others question it. To you, variety is the spice of life. You tend to keep your options open, having lots of opportunities on the go, but take care or others might consider you a bit of a flight risk in friendship.

Cunning Action: Your quick thinking allows you to get out of sticky situations. There's no shame in disengaging from a conversation or activity that you're dispassionate about. Use your analytical skills to dissect thorny situations and come up with clever solutions.

Sorcerer

Sorcerers are spellcasters whose power comes from within. You are filled with raw magic—or, in the real world, raw talent. Your talent could be anything from creative pursuits to academic ones. Whether you come from a long line of astrophysicists or you were born with an innate interest in the stars, you have unexplained talent that courses through your veins. That said, good things can always be improved upon, and trying to better understand your gifts will allow you to master them.

Metamagic: Your talents are unique to you, and as such, you can twist them to suit your needs. This fountain of energy allows you to pursue whatever path you desire whether it's creative, intellectual, or passion projects. Although you work hard, some things feel like they just come more naturally to you.

Warlock

In D&D, what sets a warlock apart from other spellcasters is their pact with an otherworldly being. Now, it's honestly your business if you want to make a pact with an eldritch horror in real life, but if that's not what you signed up for when you started reading this book, that's also perfectly acceptable. You could instead be in a mentor-and-mentee or master-and-apprentice situation. Alternatively, it could be more of an abstract ideal that you are beholden to. Whatever the case may be, you are driven by an insatiable need for knowledge and power. While you're delving into unlocking the secrets of the universe, do remember the old adage of "all work and no play . . ."

Pact Boon: Your patron (whether it is an actual person or an ideal) rewards your loyalty with a gift. In the real world, consider it the thing that helps you to achieve your goals. Is it a bullet journal for increasing your productivity, an emotional support animal that provides comfort, or maybe it's your tools of trade? Treat the gift with respect and it'll serve you well.

Wizard

Wizards live and die by a search for knowledge. You are a scholar who wants to master the mysteries of the world. While in the real world this could mean you're a librarian or scientist, it could also simply mean you believe that knowledge is power. You improve your skills through intense study and practice and can be a diligent perfectionist. There's a fine line between working hard on a team and becoming a monstrous control freak who tries to do everyone else's job for them.

Magic Missile: This spell does damage without having to roll to see if it hits or misses. In real life, you're a sure shot when it comes to facts. All that book learning means you're brimming with information, and you maintain high standards of how to do something the right way.

Class Compatibility

Once you have a better understanding of your class, you probably want to know how well you play with others. With this chart, you can find out if you and someone you know are soul mates, best friends, or . . . a recipe for disaster. Never fear, though—even opposites can attract! You'll find more details below about how well you get along (or don't) with different classes in life. Of course, there are always going to be exceptions to rules. The classes here have been broken down into personality types. Think of them like the D&D equivalent of zodiac signs.

	Barbarian	Bard	Cleric	Druid	Fighter
Barbarian				♦	♦
Bard		♦			O
Cleric					♦
Druid	♦			♦	X
Fighter	♦	O	♦	X	
Monk	X	♦	O	♦	
Paladin	♦	O		♦	O
Ranger	O				♦
Rogue	♦		O		
Sorcerer	O		X		♦
Warlock		♦		O	
Wizard		X		O	

Legend: O = compatible, ◆ = favorable, X = unfavorable

Monk	Paladin	Ranger	Rogue	Sorcerer	Warlock	Wizard
X	◆	O	◆	O		
◆	O				◆	X
O			O	X		
◆	◆				O	O
	O	◆		◆		
		◆	O	◆		
			◆		X	
◆			X	O		◆
O	◆	X	◆			◆
◆		O				
	X				◆	O
		◆	◆		O	

Barbarian: Your need for adventure, passion, and competition makes the ranger and sorcerer ideal companions. What you share in common with a ranger is a desire to make life experiences of your own. You are both explorers and pioneers who don't like to waste time simply reading about it or listening to others talk about theirs. A sorcerer is extremely dynamic and enjoys life to the fullest, so you might be the only ones able to keep up with one another's intensity. Conversely, a monk's approach to life is quite different from yours. Where you need space to burn brightly, a monk may not see eye to eye with your blunt approach to life and thrill-seeking tendencies.

Bard: Known for your enchanting creativity, a bard's raison d'être is to create human connections. Bards also love to be in love. You'll likely find it extremely grounding to be around a paladin, who can be tolerant and sympathetic. A paladin's stable view of life can hold you afloat from being carried away by romantic idealism. Another great match is a fighter who can provide a steadfast foundation for your idealism. While a fighter is often caught up in their own plans, that can easily be forgiven since you tend to withdraw into your own mind, too. You might find a wizard has too many different objectives from you to form any kind of meaningful relationship. Your dreamy nature might irritate a wizard while you might find a wizard to be too methodical.

Cleric: You are deeply motivated by the spirit of egalitarianism. A monk just seems to get you, and this creates a strong foundation from which to build a lasting relationship of any sort. In fact, you share more similarities than differences, and this creates a harmonious balance. Although it may come as a surprise, a rogue can make for an unconventional relationship. Rogues look at and experience the world in a practical way, and you can be drawn together by intellectual magnetism. Besides which, you can be amused and sip tea together while enjoying the reactions of those who are surprised by your relationship. Sorcerers, on the other hand, may do things just to get a rise out of you, and that may prove taxing on any relationship. Meanwhile, your strong, righteous convictions make you more obstinate in the face of their capricious nature.

Druid: You enjoy relaxing in serene environments, whether it's in your garden or at a spa. But you're also not afraid to roll up your sleeves and work hard, which is why you have a lot in common with a warlock. Both of you have a strong work ethic and a true-to-self nature. While this relationship might look a little boring on the outside, it will stand the test of time. Likewise, a wizard is another class that tends to work well alongside you. There's a lot of groundedness and real talk that goes into this very practical relationship. Together you can power through any obstacles. You might want to give a fighter a wide berth, though, as you both have very distinct ideas for how a project should be completed and aren't great at listening to others. When together, expect clashes from which neither of you will back down.

Fighter: Under your tough exterior, you have a passionate heart. A bard intuitively gets that about you, and you are drawn to their dreamy, passionate, and creative energy. No matter how tough life is, you can always find solace and attention in a bard. In a paladin, you'll find someone who has common goals that run much deeper than just getting their work done and taking home a paycheck. A paladin wants to mean something to the world, and what comes out of a relationship between a fighter and a paladin is net positive for everyone involved. Success comes when you put your minds together to solve common problems. One relationship that may be so fraught with troubles before it begins is with a druid. They can be slow to get moving, and you'll likely find they clash with your relentless desire for control.

Monk: With your focus on balance and harmony, you strive to create equilibrium in all areas of life. In a cleric, you'll find a true kindred spirit. This relationship is marked with a lot of lengthy and profound conversations. Together you have a philosophical approach to life where both forces are committed to changing humanity as a whole. While it may seem unlikely, a rogue can also combine forces to achieve a harmonious balance and lasting relationship. Some things get better with time. If you use the gifts of your personality traits wisely together, you can both excel. There's no competition here, so everyone is assured of equal accountability and equal benefit. A relationship with a barbarian, however, can be extremely challenging. There is an inherent polarity between you. In fact, you're 180 degrees apart. Where a barbarian is impulsive, excitable, and ready to jump right into something new and exciting, you are peace-loving and prefer a calm, smooth approach to life.

Paladin: You are an empathetic protector who can sense what others need, often long before they have articulated it themselves. In a fighter, you'll be quick to recognize the kindred spirit. You generally see eye to eye and understand each other very well. Your mutual determination makes this relationship one of formidable strength. You make a powerful team when you agree on your goals. If you can work out your initial differences, a bard complements and harmonizes with you very well. You're both dreamers in your own ways. While you are very self-driven and motivated, a bard walks their own path, and together this makes for a multifaceted relationship, whereas a warlock lives in a completely different world from you. You may find them perpetually preoccupied, which can test your patience.

Ranger: You are always on a quest and ready to launch many of your life's pursuits like blazing arrows, chasing after your next adventure. With a barbarian, you're guaranteed continuous excitement on account of your daring natures. Your mutual love for an exciting and adventurous life allows you to be pioneers as you take the path that is left untrodden. Likewise, a sorcerer has a lot of energy and the initiative to get things done. While they like to take charge and you take the time to survey a situation, the nuances of difference in your approach to life means there's never a dull moment. You can encourage each other to aim high! Unfortunately, a rogue has wildly different ideas as to how to obtain life's answers. You may find yourselves fighting about who's in charge, and you both have competitive streaks that can flare up at inopportune moments.

Rogue: You are interested in so many life pursuits you sometimes wish you could clone yourself just to get everything done. So, it's easy for you to admire a monk's ability to balance everything. In fact, you can expose each other to new and different points of view and areas of interest and help each other open up your worlds. You can have a lot of fun exploring many new ideas together. Perhaps surprisingly, you can also work really well with a cleric when you're aligned. A cleric is a humanitarian thinker while you are a doer,

so there are a lot of successful projects and adventures you can pursue together as you both offer each other different approaches to life. Some differences are challenging to bridge, though, as is the case with a ranger. Sparks might fly—and not in a good way. This relationship could turn into a forest fire!

Sorcerer: You have boundless talent with a take-charge attitude. A ranger shares a lot of common ground with you. It's likely you'll appreciate how easygoing they are and up for any adventure. With their "anything goes" mentality, you're sure to have lots of spontaneous road trips and travel plans. Similarly, a barbarian shares your passionate and spontaneous nature. You have a genuine admiration and respect for each other. With your equally large personalities, you'll need to learn to take turns commanding and giving orders even when it's picking what Netflix series to binge. The stubborn convictions of a cleric can cause things to go a bit awry in a relationship with them. There are likely to be a lot of challenges due to your differences and fixed natures, which can lead each to get stuck in your groove and bring on open warfare with each other.

Warlock: You can tap into your inner strength to overcome whatever stands between you and your long-term goals; don't let anything distract you from getting ahead. A druid gets all that. They prefer calm over chaos. With their "slow and steady wins the race" mentality, together you'll have a relationship that knows the value of persistence and taking initiative. You'll also find a wizard shares a lot of your interests. You're both practical, ambitious, and hardworking, plus you understand the value of working hard to create a good life. This is a relationship that radiates with magical awesomeness. Conversely, a paladin might think of you as a cold know-it-all or workaholic, so focused and ambitious that you forget about personal relationships. Compromise here can be difficult, so you might be better served looking elsewhere for a relationship.

Wizard: You are a perfectionist at heart and aren't afraid to improve skills through diligent and consistent practice. A druid knows nothing good will come without putting in the effort. Because you both have a practical, realistic view of the world and share a lot of the same core values, you can be assured of a quiet but comfortable relationship if you're willing to take the time to nurture one. A warlock is someone you can hold conversations with on any topic. You're both old souls, and though your relationship is practical and predictable, it's also pretty unshakable. On the opposite side of things, a bard has a vastly different personality from yours, and you might find their "head in the clouds" nature frustrating. Meanwhile, your tendency to be a little overly critical, even if you are just joking around, might wound their ego.

The various classes have a lot to offer both in the game and in your everyday life. By identifying with a class, you gain more insight into how to move forward on your adventure. It helps you highlight your strengths and helps you identify who can best support you on your quests. Some ways you can test your compatibility with other classes is seeing what kinds of activities you each enjoy, where your interests intersect, and how well you do some of them together. Here are some examples to get you started.

COMPATIBILITY ACTIVITIES

d20	Activity
1–2	Trivia night at a pub
3–4	A fine-dining experience
5–6	Hiking
7–8	Comedy club
9–10	Spa day
11–12	Trip to a botanical garden
13–14	Taking an art class together
15–16	Yoga
17–18	Skydiving
19–20	A home-cooked meal

In the next chapter, you'll learn how to take a step back as a PC and dive behind the screen as a Dungeon Master. Will you learn how to manipulate time and space? You'll have to read on to find out!

PART 3

BE THE DUNGEON MASTER OF YOUR LIFE

6

THE BIG
PICTURE

In a way, everyone is Dungeon Master (DM) of their own life. Think about it: you control many of the aspects of what you do, who you interact with, and the general path your life will take. Because the DM plays such a crucial role in D&D, it only feels appropriate that this role is given the treatment it deserves by doing a deep dive into what it means to be the best DM you can be. And, no, even though you are kind of all-seeing and mostly all-knowing during a D&D campaign, it doesn't mean you're *a god*. Instead, the DM is the person who creates the worlds and stories within which the PCs play, feeling supported and challenged in equal measure. So, what does that mean? As the DM, either in a D&D game or in your life, it means you're a leader. You are creative, flexible, and interested in working with others to help them reach goals. In this chapter, we're going to explore the many aspects of a DM, and how to use these skills to help make your life more enjoyable.

DUNGEON MASTER

A DM serves three main roles in D&D: referee, narrator, and playing the other roles (villain, monsters, and NPCs). They adjudicate the rules, collaborate on storytelling, and create interesting villains and support characters. Anyone can be the DM, but it generally falls to the one in the group who enjoys herding cats, er, players. Two things that are essential for a good DM: (1) They make sure everyone is having fun—even if that means bending the rules a bit. (2) They ensure that everything is fair.

Being a Dungeon Master is a job that comes with a lot of responsibilities, one of them being the person who organizes and arranges a world for other people. In your day-to-day life, your *players* can be friends, family, coworkers, or anyone else you interact with closely on a regular basis, and your *world* is the spaces in which you all intersect and inhabit together, whether that's your house or a workspace or your favorite hangout. You might be thinking, *Do I have what it takes to be a Dungeon Master?* Well, let's think about some of the skills that you already have. When you are in a situation where you have to manage a group of people, a good DM tries to inspire, motivate, and encourage those around them. This could mean ensuring everyone feels they have a place at the table to share their thoughts, or knowing when to push and challenge the group, or being a thoughtful mediator.

Remember, being a DM is not simply about you or what you can bring to the table but, instead, how to support others to bring all *they* can to the table as well. Whether your players are trying to defeat a gelatinous cube or just trying to brainstorm the next big thing, as long as you are being thoughtful, supportive, and creative, you have what it takes to be a DM. Of course, it is important to ensure that you are fostering a safe, supportive space for your players to interact in and an engaging world or problems to challenge them, but we have only begun to scratch the surface of what makes a good DM.

The DM Roles

There are lots of hats that a DM wears, but they can be compart-mentalized into four key roles: architect, performer, manager, and appraiser. Every DM is as unique as their players, but you'll likely find you balance these roles in varying combinations, depending on your style. If you're low-prep, you probably don't put a lot of emphasis on the architect role, but it's still a part of what you do—otherwise, your story falls apart. Likewise, you may not think of yourself as a performer if you don't put on accents, but you're still entertaining your players.

Dear Tasha,

How do I figure out what kind of Dungeon Master I am when it comes to applying these skills to my actual life?

—Desperate to DM

When it comes to bending reality, you really couldn't have chosen someone better to come to with your predicament. I'm told a Dungeon Master is all-powerful, which sounds like an exaggeration to me. Perhaps Volo wrote that entry on DMs. In any case, the role isn't as mystical as you might make it out to be. After all, magic on Earth is rather . . . mundane. But I did grow up in a house with chicken legs, so what do I know?

You and your friends want to take on the role of heroes—or charming anti-heroes (who can blame them?)—and go forth on adventures. Not to conquer dragons but to achieve goals that don't involve evading a breath weapon. Wise choice since you're occupying a human body now! How do you direct the cosmos to your every whim, you ask? Oh, you didn't ask that? That's right, you wanted to know how to find your DM style. The best advice I can offer is to practice each role. Find what fits right. Like shopping for a witch's hat, it's not one size fits all. Also, use the resources you have available, such as your companions, who likely have all sorts of opinions and preferences when it comes to how to organize them. The mundane magic of the "internet" is also helpful for gleaning information about personality types, managing other humans, putting on fun voices, and so on.

So, let the dice land where they may. However, if you're not having fun at any given time during your quest, adjust. Nothing's written in stone, and fate can be rewound with powerful enough spells. When things don't go your way, adjust your approach. If all else fails, you can always hurl the world into another plane of existence and start from scratch.

—Tasha

The Architect

One way to think of a DM is as an architect who builds from a strong foundation. And what exactly do you design? *Experience.* In game, a DM looks for the story beats so that no matter where the characters wind up, they'll hit certain milestones. As an architect, planning in this way has useful applications in real life. Think of it like an outline or a road map for laying out a few different options of how things can go in a group plan. You can keep a similar list for meetings or to help prioritize things during the day. That way, you can focus your attention on what needs to be done.

When leading a campaign, an architect will have notes, backup plans, and tons of great NPCs to interact with their PCs, but they also will have created a story or situation that encourages (or challenges) each of their players to test their limits and discover something new about themselves. An architect always looks at the big picture and considers what everyone else is going to get out of the experience or the situation.

To better embrace your inner architect, it often helps if you take the time to think through your goals, expectations, and priorities because this level of planning often helps to relieve some of the mental burden of trying to keep track of everything you'd like to in the moment. It's always a good idea to know all the details pertinent to the issue at hand or the context of the situation you're in from work presentations, dungeon mapping, or planning a road trip with a group of friends. Of course, just because you are leaning into your architect nature, that doesn't mean you have to do all the planning on your own. In fact, the mark of a great DM, no matter your roles or styles, is your ability to collaborate from the start.

The Performer

So, after you build the foundation for your plan, you need to be able to sell it to your team or group. How you deliver news, content, and information often has a direct impact on how well it's received. And let's not forget that what you choose to share is equally as important as *how* you share it, which is sometimes much easier to do when you know who your players are.

ON YOUR TURN

Before you ever roll dice in a game, a good idea is to have what's called Session 0. This is where the DM and players sit down around the table to discuss expectations by talking about the type of experience everyone is interested in having with the game. In the case of any real-life undertaking with a group of people, it is crucial that everyone is involved and should feel like their comments and suggestions are being heard and respected.

Individuals are, well, unique, and since a group is made up of a whole bunch of individuals, it's important to remember that each Session 0 can look very different—even with the same group of people. These same principles apply to team building, friendship cultivating, and so much more.

With this information in hand, you have a better understanding and can be respectful of personal likes and dislikes. Plus, being able to answer questions like "How often do you want to meet?" and "Are there topics of discussion that are off-limits?" It's a great way to build a solid foundation for your group. So, if one of your friends wants to hit up the insect museum while you're on vacation together, but your other friend, Drizzt, has confided in you about his arachnophobia, you can champion splitting the party for an afternoon.

And what if you've never had a real-life Session 0? Of course, a check-in meeting is always a good idea. Even if you think you know the people in your life, sometimes they change. Following up from time to time to ensure everyone is still on the same page is a great way to show you care and to update your mental contact card.

A common misconception is that people think that *performing* means putting on fun voices or bringing drama to the table. Certainly, that is a really helpful and fun aspect that DMs can bring to their games to help their players feel more immersed in the story and the world, but there is more to it than that. For example, maybe you want to pitch a team-building retreat at work. Your success is going to be determined by how well you present the points that will sell the leaders and decision-makers in a group on the idea, without losing any of the appeal—no one wants to go on a *boring* retreat—that will resonate with your various coworkers who will need to attend. Hey, nobody said being a DM was an easy task. That's why there's a whole chapter dedicated to them!

Anyway, at its most basic level, performing is about how you present information—and ideally it's in a way that is interesting and engaging to your audience. In a campaign, sometimes that means donning an accent or voice for an important NPC, and in the real world, sometimes it means preparing a visual presentation to help elaborate your points, including the hard-hitting numbers about how work retreats improve collaboration and sense of workplace culture, plus a great list of all the activities and events that you'll do together.

The Manager

A DM is the one responsible for getting a group of people to come together and work toward a common goal. Teamwork is critical, but sometimes it is equally important to have someone there to manage the group. Helping your players be supportive team members and effectively collaborating with one another is an important skill, and being prepared and knowing how to present the right information at the right time are

two elements that can help you accomplish this. Your job is to guide everyone so that they are on the same page and have a solid idea of how they might work together to accomplish the task at hand.

In fact, even the best leaders know when to take a step back and give others an opportunity to shine. In D&D, a DM is there as someone to listen and react to the needs of their players but also to give them the space to grow, learn, and take charge in the story, so good DMs will give their players opportunities to lead and direct the flow of action in a way that feels organic and compatible to them. A great DM offers opportunities for players to engage with things beyond their PCs and can offer players control of NPCs or collaboration on elements of world-building itself.

In your day-to-day DMing, there are many reasons and scenarios where you might want to let others take a turn in the driver's seat, including when delegating projects or relying on someone else's exper-

tise. Both of these examples are ways that you can empower the people around you to make important decisions and share their knowledge by letting them know that you trust and respect their wisdom and authority. After all, just because you're good at leading people doesn't mean you have a naturally high Wisdom modifier. Remember, you don't have a *Dungeon Master's Guide* to life, the universe, and everything. During a campaign, another reason to let someone else guide the group is because that person is learning to be a DM themselves. Taking on a mentoring role is also something that is just as likely to happen in your day-to-day life as well, and a good leader doesn't feel threatened by the talents or ambitions of others.

Of course, these aren't the only reasons to let someone else lead, but they are really great examples of scenarios where you can start. And there doesn't always need to be a reason! Sometimes it is just nice to give those around you the opportunities to grow or challenge themselves, so just be willing to offer up the reins to the caravan every once in a while and see where someone might take you and the group.

And yes, even when you are always working for a consensus and are being mindful of teamwork opportunities, and just enjoying the fun you're having, there will be times when you can't come to a decision that wholly satisfies everyone. But, hey, you're taking inspiration from D&D, so in the worst-case scenario or as a last resort, just remember you could always roll some dice. Or check out a random decision-maker online or create a random decision table with the help of the group because, let's face it, sometimes you can't make everyone happy—and that's okay. As long as everyone agrees to accept the outcome and at least most everyone walks away from the situation feeling that their opinion has been heard and some middle ground has been met, then you're doing just fine.

The Appraiser

Finally, a DM is someone who is constantly assessing and reassessing a situation, as well as the mood and dynamics of their players and their characters. Just like in a campaign, a group's dynamic can often change throughout the course of the day or over a much longer period of time. Maybe some of your players have started to take the spotlight far too often, or someone engages in behavior that makes the experience less fun for others. Real-life drama happens, but a good DM tries to find ways for disruptive people to realize their mutual goals can only be achieved through cooperation. More than that, a DM is always checking in, actively listening, and communicating directly with the group during every step of the way. Remember Session 0? The rule is *things change*, so it's important to keep your finger on the pulse of the group and adjust as needed.

And when something completely out of the blue happens? You need to be flexible and adaptable, using your knowledge and experience to manage those random unexpected moments and situations effectively. When you can face challenges quickly and decisively, it helps your group, your players, or your team learn to depend on and trust you when things take a turn.

By appraising certain situations, you're also able to make connections and gather information that will help you when considering whether players have something—be it an idea, an item, a spare umbrella, or a good bit of advice or experience—that might be of value or could benefit the group as a whole. Maybe you have a friend who just moved to the city and is looking for some new people to connect with, and you've been waiting for the right time to introduce them to some of your other friends. Or perhaps your bardic friend has just released their first album and you happen to know someone at a radio station who curates new music. Connections can be big or small, but as a DM, you're always looking for opportunities to help make them happen.

The Master of Ceremonies

As you can see, the DM wears a lot of different hats, but the common thread that runs throughout their many tasks, roles, and responsibilities is that they are someone who leads others. To some extent, that means that you're a people person and you thrive on human interactions, which allow groups to achieve their best, but that isn't a hard-and-fast rule. There are definitely more quiet or shy DMs who are just as capable, thoughtful, and supportive as a more outgoing DM. As long as you are someone who is flexible, understanding—being creative doesn't hurt either—and open to helping others learn and grow, then you are a DM.

Some goals, like some campaigns, are long-term and require the occasional boost in motivation, so remember that acknowledging and appreciating your group's efforts will go a long way. Being perceptive and taking the time to reward and recognize the people you work (or create or even live) with is the mark of a great DM, plus knowing what motivates your team, players, friends, and family doesn't hurt either. Whether it's a small gesture, like a pat on the back, a small gift, or something else you know they'll appreciate, incentives (a.k.a. treasures) are always helpful in building stronger relationships—and they are really fun, too. Nurturing your relationships is critical to continued success. Just be sure to not go overboard. Even the *Dungeon Master's Guide* has tables for rewards based on levels. You don't need to buy a new car for your teenager just because they remembered to take the garbage out!

Make sure you don't forget to check out the Dungeon Master section on your character sheet on page 141 and fill out your DM role and skills.

7
FORMING AN ADVENTURING PARTY

The unique (and kind of genius) thing about D&D is that, for even the most combat-driven party, the game is still all about social interactions. After all, the whole point of the game is that you sit around a table with a group of friends (or online as incorporeal voices or images on a screen) and collaborate on ways to solve various conflicts and problems within the context of a fictional world. Whether it's with friends, family, coworkers, or even a group of strangers at a convention, you're socializing. It's these interactions with the other PCs and NPCs in your life that make up a good portion of your day-to-day existence.

Though, unfortunately, the biggest difference between the D&D world and the real one is that you don't generally get do-overs. So, if you blurt out, "I hate everything about this," during a business presentation, you don't have the benefit of an understanding DM who can ask, "Do you say that out loud?" And not even a stellar saving throw can help you now. Instead, you have to accept that you just stepped in a steaming pile of real-world owlbear poop . . . and maybe made the environment at your workplace a little more hostile to boot.

So, how do you navigate social situations with the various NPCs of your life? With a bit of bardic inspiration and brushing up your Charisma skills! This chapter covers topics like communication skills, where to meet like-minded adventurers, and how to support one another so you can be your best questing selves.

Charisma Check

Being an active listener (learn more about this on page 28) and practicing good communication skills can improve your life because, well, people make up a good portion of the world. Unless you're a hermit, off-grid in the deep woods somewhere, then you're probably going to have to communicate or interact with other people at least a few times a day. Much like when you are playing a character in D&D, a good measure of your social intelligence can be determined by how self-aware you are about your interactions with others. You can level up by socializing and communicating with others—be they a partner, coworker, friend, or fellow party member—and learn from successes and failures that you might have in an interpersonal setting. Speaking in D&D terms, most of the building blocks of social intelligence are Charisma-based, like being self-aware, as well as the ability to self-regulate and manage relationships. However, there's also a bit of Perception thrown in because it's helpful being able to read a room and tell when your party member (or partner) says they aren't upset about the fact that you ate the last piece of cheesecake—but you know they really are because, you know, what kind of monster does that even?

DM STATE OF MIND

Let's get real meta for a moment here. Have you ever been in a game of D&D and just zoned out from the conversation for a moment whether through inattention or distraction? Or the reverse, where you've been describing a scene or narrating your actions, and it seems like nobody really heard what you were saying? Active listening is a prime example of social intelligence that you need to foster positive relationships.

Now, let's reimagine the situation: You're gathered around the table and a player is going into great detail about their character's turn action when a text message pops up on your phone from your partner. What do you do?

a. Take a peek at the text—it seems like the player is going to be a while.
b. Continue to pay attention and read the text later.
c. Covertly respond to the text while nodding and attempting to look engaged.

If you answered *b*, you'd be correct. While a momentary distraction may seem fine on the surface, you're not treating others in a way you'd want to be treated. Getting caught not listening to another person you're in a conversation with is socially awkward for a reason. You might internalize panic and attempt to cover up your inattentiveness, but the damage is usually already done. We all slip up, so definitely give yourself a break if it happens occasionally.

In D&D, and in life, communication is the best policy. Had a rough day and feel like you aren't giving someone your full attention, or are you waiting for some important news to come your way? Tell those around you. If you are at the table, share what is going on and offer to build in more breaks during the game or politely ask for a moment to step away.

Also, if focusing for long periods of time is challenging for you, discuss this with your group. Maybe the group will help incorporate more opportunities for each person to interact. In a family or work setting, it may be ensuring each person gets opportunities to speak. In a D&D session, perhaps the DM will create more situations for the players to describe their characters' actions.

In fact, other members of your group may have similar challenges, and by speaking up, you'll open the door for their benefit, too.

How to Win Friends (and Influence NPCs)

So, how *do* you win friends and influence NPCs? Just like in D&D, the people you meet in life will have a certain first impression or baseline attitude toward you, and they, generally speaking, will fall into one of three categories: friendly, indifferent, or hostile. This means that, as you go about your day and interact with people, you're essentially making Charisma checks against these impressions or attitudes of the people around you. A Charisma check is like reading the room and trying to determine the likelihood of how well your words or actions will go over with the people around you. Anything from telling a joke at a party, trying to get a better deal on a car, trying to make an impression during a job interview or first date, or convincing your roommate or partner to order pizza instead of Thai for dinner, and the list goes on and on.

Of course, some tasks are easier than others. As with any skill check, you'll have a sort of level that you need to overcome to succeed; in D&D, it's known as Difficulty Class (DC). DC is applied to any task that's not a straight success or considered "easy," so it could apply to putting together IKEA furniture or persuading someone to believe you truly weren't laughing at them. Some are easy, like choosing a movie to watch with a group of close friends, while others are more difficult, like trying to convince Tika from marketing that no, you didn't actually hate everything about her presentation. By navigating these situations, you can gain advantage on these types of skill checks because the more you interact with people, the more proficient you'll become in various social interactions. But the key here is "more and more interaction," which basically means that it takes practice.

Let's just be honest and up-front now: you aren't going to know how to navigate every situation, and you are going to make mistakes or do or say things that are going to change someone's attitude or impression of you. It sucks, but it's the truth. That said, a lot of social situations can be made a little easier when you are being sincere, honest, and authentic and are showing genuine interest in and respect for another person—especially if you don't see eye to eye. Of course, this isn't going to work on villains who are out to live their best (worst?) lives, and no amount of persuasion or honest conversation is going to change that.

So, yes, tricky social situations are going to come up. When you're navigating a tricky social situation, it's especially important to remember that people are emotional creatures. If you go on the offense, expect defensiveness. If you're going to be critical, pinpoint the cause and effect without dragging someone down (you can also learn more about effective communication on page 20). Otherwise, you might fail that Charisma check and wind up messing up the punch line of your joke, not getting the deal on that car, botching the job interview, and . . . well, you get the picture.

You Meet at a Tavern

One of the most common tropes in D&D is meeting at a tavern, where an NPC gives you a quest. But outside of a real-life tavern, how do you meet new people and gain new experiences? That would be by networking. If that sounds a little too business-y, rest assured that networking isn't something that just happens in a professional work setting. Technically, anything that gets you out of the house and interacting with someone can be considered a networking opportunity. And, yes, D&D counts! So does a book club or a running group or . . . a networking event.

In a D&D session, an NPC often sends an adventuring party on a quest, but what reason do they have to approach a level 1 adventuring party? Unless it's a scam, they probably heard of you because you have a reputation. The same is true in your daily life—you are much more likely to connect with a book club if you have a "reputation" of frequenting the same local bookshop and reading the same graphic novels and fantasy books, or more likely to get hired to manage the community garden if you have a "reputation" for tending large gardens like this in the past. That's also where real-life networking comes into play because, by getting to know someone better, you are bound to find ways to help each other either in the present or the future. Take the example of trying to join a book club. By getting to know the owner of the shop and getting into some great discussions about the latest graphic novel by a popular author, they might ask if you are interested in being introduced to the host of the book club.

The goal of networking, at its very core, is to build relationships with the people around you—sometimes based on similar interests that you might share or communities that you might belong to. By doing so, you also gain a positive reputation in your community. Always remember that, unlike quests, networking is a two-way street, so don't be selfish or self-serving.

Often networking is associated with either professional or more formal social events and networks because it is sometimes much easier, and more common, to develop those kinds of relationships and communities in that context. This setting or type of network might also just come easier to some than others because it is supported or required as part of someone's job—no one is requiring you to network with your fellow local druids. There are also those who sometimes might seem like they have the advantage when it comes to networking, whether that means having family, friends, or a community who are able to help them make connections, while there are others who might seem more naturally charismatic and outgoing.

Just remember, at its very core, networking is about hanging out and enjoying the company of other people, communicating your interests, and connecting with others who share those interests. Of course, it's easier to do in certain situations—depending on who you are—whether that is meeting people at a special, more niche event rather than a broad professional one or one-on-one over coffee rather than on social media.

Just like in D&D, you can't assess what level another PC or NPC is on sight alone. It's possible that the CEO of a company wears a Saint Laurent suit, or maybe she's a twenty-eight-year-old with rainbow hair. The point is: you should try to treat everyone you come across as an equal.

And when you do strike up a conversation with someone new—and especially when it seems like you are really hitting it off—make it your quest to discover what makes them unique or where you share common ground. People generally love to talk about themselves, so this shouldn't be too hard—unless you like to talk about yourself, too. Don't forget that your effort goes a long way, especially appreciated with shy people who may need someone in their corner at an event (or online, with their permission, of course). And if you're the shy person trying to network, just make that first connection and then ask them if they would feel comfortable introducing you to other people they might have met or being your networking wingman. Also, there isn't anything wrong with making one connection either. Just go at a pace that feels comfortable to you because networking should be a positive and enjoyable experience!

On Your Turn

Interactions with new NPCs can seem daunting, but with practice, it becomes easier. Some simple networking tips can go a long way when attempting to forge connections while on this quest called life. Remember, networking can be any activity where you're able to meet people who may be able to help each other out in some way, whether it's in forming friendships, business opportunities, or romantic relationships.

1. Be human. While you could try to channel your inner elf or firbolg, you'll want to focus on making authentic connections, which means being true to who you really are.
2. Be strategic. What talents, strengths, skill sets, and connections can you bring to the table? Map out things you like to talk about!
3. Be a good listener. Enough said, literally.

The Heroic Buffs of D&D

If you're good with people—and it is a skill that takes practice to be proficient at—you can more easily avoid being with the people you don't jibe with. When you do start making connections, you'll probably want to maintain them. Expressing your appreciation for NPCs or members of your adventuring party in real life is the surest way to ensure they know how you feel. That's where your knowledge of them comes into play. Everyone wants to feel cared for and appreciated, but each person values different ways of communicating all that. It's not quite love languages, but here's a breakdown of the "support" languages of D&D:

Quest Taking: Has your partner or roommate bemoaned the killer dust bunny of Caerbannog that dwells deep beneath the household furniture? If they're someone who appreciates gestures, taking on this quest to banish (i.e., vacuum) this creature out of existence is the way to go.

Treasure Giving: Give them that sweet loot! This might seem like it's pretty straightforward, but it helps to know what the receiver prefers—maybe a gift card at their favorite tea shop so they can pick out the specific item, or perhaps they prefer a handmade card to show you put more work into the gift.

Inspiring Words: Regardless of whether you have proficiency in Charisma skill checks or took a related feat, an authentic compliment goes a long way. Some people just want to hear that you appreciate them.

Downtime Together: Hit up the beach and conquer the, um, waves? The person who enjoys downtime with you is just looking for the experience of hanging out with you to know you made the time for them.

Magic Touch: It could be a pat on the back for a job well done or a hug (twenty seconds is optimal, according to science), but you've got the magic touch when it comes to people who prefer physical contact. So high-five away, but remember consent is always key when this kind of contact is involved.

Identifying well with others leads to more relationships and potentially more friendships. If you know their likes, you have a better chance of growing and maintaining a healthy network of people in your life. Pretty soon, you'll have all sorts of NPCs on your side to help you (and your adventuring party) achieve your goals. And when you have your whole squad together, you're set to start on a campaign!

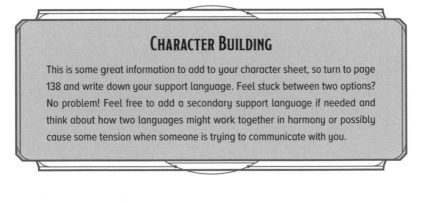

CHARACTER BUILDING

This is some great information to add to your character sheet, so turn to page 138 and write down your support language. Feel stuck between two options? No problem! Feel free to add a secondary support language if needed and think about how two languages might work together in harmony or possibly cause some tension when someone is trying to communicate with you.

PART 4

ADVENTURING

8

THE CAMPAIGN
CALLED LIFE

Okay, you've learned what class matches you outside the Forgotten Realms, you're a little more prepared for what randomness life throws at you, and, hey, you've got your phone, wallet, and a spell scroll, just in case (and if you haven't, then check out Chapter 4 for classes and Chapter 3 for dealing with life, on pages 48 and 34). Looks like you're ready for your first adventure! So, what do you want to do or accomplish?

In D&D, your adventures usually have objectives and obstacles that are often woven into the story to help guide the players, and they are pretty clear-cut, so they know what the ultimate goal is. Those objective and obstacles can be big moments or important tasks, like fighting the dragon that's been terrorizing a village. Or they can be smaller moments that are included throughout the journey to help keep things interesting or because, well, someone should do them, like going on a fetch quest to help out an NPC. The same goes for your daily life. You can have larger objectives like acing an entrance exam, moving to a new city, or taking that work opportunity and smaller ones like going to the grocery store, meeting up with a friend, or treating yourself to some quality downtime.

And you can (and should) embrace as many of these objectives and obstacles that you'll come across in life because that's what makes the adventure so exciting and fun. While some of life's objectives and obstacles will be random occurrences or opportunities, many, like the ones above, are often already part of your daily routine or general life. With those, we can think of both objectives and obstacles as tasks and goals that you want to accomplish. In this chapter, we are going to look at how you can view your goals through the lens of D&D objectives and use your passions, talents, and drive with your unique set of skills and abilities to help you achieve them.

A Quest Called Life

Having goals and working toward them is an important part of life. Goals give a sense of purpose while also keeping things interesting and engaging on your adventure. Of course, the path to achieving those goals may include a few detours or a kobold ambush, and sometimes we step off the path to take on a side quest or to just explore, but the great thing about goals is that they are always going to be there and they aren't set in stone. Goals, like people, can change or shift with a person as they learn and grow.

And, before reading further, let's clarify what we mean by *goals*. By no means do these have to be massive, earth-shattering "quests." While they can be long-term goals, like creating your own tech startup, they can also be short-term goals, like paying off your credit cards in the next year, or even stepping-stone goals, like setting a budget for yourself. So, grab a snack and get out there and work toward your goals!

Planning Your Quests

We all know that sometimes establishing and working toward your goals are often easier said than done—much like that plan to sneak past a beholder—often because there are outside factors that can impact your ability to achieve them. For example, maybe you want to exercise more, but it is difficult to find spare time in your day because of all your other obligations. Or maybe you want to camp at every national park. One question tends to loom in the back of your mind: How can I even do this? Fear not, and remember, most adventurers don't just delve into a dungeon without a plan (unless that is kind of your thing; sorry, fighters and rogues), and the same applies to your various quests (goals) in life—plus you have this book to help you.

So, when you are eager to take on a quest (any quest, you aren't picky) or have a quest in mind, but maybe aren't sure how to get started in pursuing it, here are six steps that can help you!

1. **Cast the die.** First, figure out what kind of quest you want. Think about what story you want to tell with your actions or some things that you'd like to learn about yourself. It could be that you want to make a career change or start a side business. And, if you want to go really big picture you can think about what kind of legacy you want to leave behind, but, um, maybe you should start with baby steps. Quests and goals are more fun when you choose something that truly interests you and not something you are doing to impress someone else.

    Also, thinking of a goal that will slightly challenge you is a great move because who wants a quest that is so easy you can do it in your sleep? No one, that's who. Remember, giving yourself room to grow and learn is a great motivator. So set a challenge rating (CR) for yourself that is at least a level above "cruise control."

2. **Put it on your character sheet.** If you want to stick to a plan, it helps to write it down. When an adventurer is asked to take up a quest, an NPC doesn't simply say, "Go fetch the flower." There is a fair bit of information about the quest, like who is the quest giver and why they want the flower, what kind of flower it is, and what kind of incentive is being offered in exchange for the flower. Be a good quest giver and give yourself enough information to achieve your goal.

Start by asking yourself questions. How will you know when this life quest has been achieved? Is it a number, a feeling, something else? What is your incentive for taking on this quest? Then write it all down—and be specific! "I want to cook more at home" is vague and is missing crucial information, so "I want to cook dinnertime meals from scratch every weekend for the month of June" is a much more defined and easier-to-understand quest. And don't forget the power of positive, actionable language. It's perfectly fine to think of what you'd like the result of your quest to be. However, "I don't want to be so stressed out anymore" is lacking general information to help guide you to act and feel that you have the skills to take on this quest. Instead, "I'd like to meditate for five minutes every day" is a very positive and doable quest.

3. Tell an NPC or party member. Sometimes quests are better with a little help, so don't be afraid to talk to someone about them! Chances are if you tell someone about your quest, you're more likely to go through with it. Also, there is nothing like a little bit of accountability to ensure that you don't accidently lose that quest journal you worked so hard on. From parents, friends, partners, or coworkers, don't forget that the people around you are your allies and they want to help and see you succeed—and they might be just the person when you need a little cheering on or can come in with a handy spell when you need assistance.

4. Plot your course of action. What are the steps you need to take to achieve your life quest? While this might seem more relevant for bigger goals, it is also quite helpful for smaller ones as well. Think of it as exploring a network of caves in D&D where you face small encounters in each one, which represent a milestone or deadline. As you progress through the caves (tackle each milestone), you get closer and closer to the final cave and the end of your quest. By breaking up your quest into smaller milestones, it can help make a larger goal feel more reasonable, and it also gives you opportunities to celebrate your successes along the way.

5. **Roll for initiative.** You can plan all you want, but at some point, you're going to have to take the first step on your journey. But sometimes taking that first step can feel a little daunting. Don't worry, you can do this! If you are having trouble, then lean on a party member or remind yourself of your incentive (bonus points if you have smaller treats and treasures planned for your milestones). Then, once you get the ball rolling, you'll have that momentum (and smaller incentives) to keep you going, especially if you planned out some of the other steps.

And if, while you're on your journey, you realize that maybe you set the CR a little too high? Don't worry, you're allowed to go back and revisit your plans or maybe even take a quick side quest to gain more experience before you continue on.

6. **Reward yourself.** When you achieve your goal, remember to take time to celebrate. You did the thing! If you had help, be sure to thank those who supported you. Also take time to reflect on any lessons you learned along the way. Then, after a short or long rest, it's time to take up another life quest!

CHARACTER BUILDING

As part of your character's journey, you can make use of an Encounter Log or Quest Sheet to help you visualize everyday tasks and obstacles as challenges or encounters that you can face and overcome. Turn to page 142 to learn how to create an Encounter Log or fill out your Quest Sheet.

Whether you might be a little lost about what you want to accomplish or you have a huge bucket list that you want to complete, it always helps to have a starting point. Remember, you're the hero of your story, so it's okay to take time to reflect on the things that make the journey around the sun exciting to you. Then, when you're ready, go accept the call to adventure on a path tailored to your goals and desires.

Complications

What is a quest without a few obstacles and complications? Most of the time, they are probably minor enough that you can simply dust off your robes, pick up your wand, and return to casting *magic missile*. However, some life setbacks are the kind that can define or redefine you, and taking critical damage and then healing from that—whether in a game or in real life—is no joke.

Whether it's through religious faith, social support, or the guidance of a professional, remember that you are not alone on your adventure, and it is always a good idea to ask for help and assistance when you need it. Often these people, along with your family, friends, and others in your adventuring party, are exactly who you need to call on so that you can work toward overcoming any obstacle or setback that comes your way. For complications and obstacles that feel more manageable, remember that you have a few great tools in your pack that can help.

Even in downtime, there can be complications. You're unable to make reservations at an upscale restaurant. The concert you want to go to is sold out. Some complications are ones you can avoid or learn from. But there are going to be some things you simply can't plan for, and that's where you can give yourself a moment to sit with the disappointment before asking yourself, "What now?"

DEAR TASHA,

I'm having a small destination wedding, and the invites were sent six months ago. We're a month away from the big day, but my bestie has suddenly brought up an argument we had years ago as an excuse to not attend.

—Friends with Cold Feet

Friendships can be as complicated as romantic relationships—which is why I can't be bothered with either. However, this isn't an episode of *Real Housewitches*, and it sounds like your closest friend has been carrying around a *bag of holding* stuffed with their feelings for years. Time appears to be of the essence here if you're to resolve this before your nuptials. You should employ a method of communication that makes you feel most at ease, whether it's by *sending stones* or casting *skywrite*, er, text message. There's always in-person too, but you might want to keep the location somewhere unbeloved in case tempers flare and there's a wild magic surge. There's nothing quite like a random spell going off in the middle of your favorite gastropub!

Be sure to stand by your feelings on the matter but keep an open mind. This is particularly true if your end goal is to keep this friend in your life. In that case, you'll want to salvage the friendship through healthy, levelheaded communication. There could be any number of reasons for this friend to bring up an old wound. Hear them out. Don't go in with a combative mindset, armed with insults and a laundry list of ways they've wronged you. Save that hexing energy for your true nemesis.

If you're unable to see eye to eye, at least you gave it the old spell school try and possibly avoided awkwardness on your special day!

—**Tasha**

Show Up to the Table: No matter how much you want to or how hard you try, you can't succeed at everything all the time. In a game of D&D, if you and your adventuring party are defeated by a monster, in the absence of a total party kill (TPK), the PCs persevere, but now the player characters are faced with how to continue from this point on. A TPK represents a severe and permanent setback unless you've got a necromancer on speed dial. Outside the fantasy world, these are difficult moments—a death in the family, a pandemic, a divorce—that leave you reeling. But remember, that no matter what, you have to keep playing the game if you're going to succeed in your quest. So, show up, bring your A game, and don't sweat the small stuff. But if you need to, take a break.

Time-Out: Sometimes you need a break to think or just process everything when you are faced with a difficult obstacle. Take the time you need to feel your feelings before you charge back into the fray. It is totally acceptable to be disappointed, but it's not good to wallow, so try to set a time limit to process your feelings before redirecting your emotional energy to a more positive path ahead.

Fail Up: Setbacks happen whether you prepare for them or not. If you messed up, accept responsibility, and learn from it. If it was a circumstance outside your control, figure out what went wrong and how to better prepare for or avoid it in the future.

No Meta-Gaming: You can't control everything that life throws at you, no more than your PC can control the encounters and obstacles that the DM has planned for them. The best thing that you can do is focus on what actions you can take or how you react and respond when facing a hurdle. It might be hard to remember this in the heat of the moment, but it's helpful to treat this obstacle for what it is: an incredible opportunity to grow.

ROLL FOR SUPPORT

The next time you find yourself in a situation where you're stumped or feeling a bit defeated, think about how your PC would react to the situation. Roll a d6 for an extra bit of wisdom from our classic adventuring party.

1. Hank, the ranger: "Don't play the blame game. Things happen for no obvious reason sometimes."
2. Eric, the fighter: "This is where you're at and you're going to deal with it head-on."
3. Diana, the bard: "Like the caterpillar and the butterfly, acknowledge the transformative power of change so you can flourish."
4. Presto, the wizard: "Draw on your inner strength and knowledge to push through."
5. Sheila, the rogue: "Give yourself some time and come back to it refreshed."
6. Bobby, the barbarian: *Primal scream*

Hopefully, you have some food for thought and maybe even a few helpful tips to make it easier for you to take on new quests and face any challenges or obstacles that come with them. Try to find meaning in the challenges you face so that they become more than just things you must overcome: a necessary element in your story and your growth. Whether you take action to redirect your course around obstacles or face them head-on is up to you.

When it comes to your goals, you can add a sense of adventure by thinking of them like part of your life's quests. You'll want to commit to seeing them through from start to finish. If you do something, do it with passion and purpose. And remember, sometimes the most challenging experiences turn out to be the ones you value most. Whether you're up against Tiamat, queen of the reservations list at an exclusive restaurant, or learning how to cook Bytopian Shepherd's Bread, your goals are worthy of your pursuit if only because they are important to you. They push you out of your comfort zone and help you grow. Just remember to enjoy the journey along the way.

9

WHEN ADVENTURE COMES KNOCKING

The life of a PC is filled with excitement and adventure. Taking the spirit of D&D and applying it to real life is essentially trying to capture that sense of adventure and apply it to things in your daily life like personal growth and relationships, as well as skills that will help you overcome challenges, help you feel more confident, or just give you a new perspective on your day-to-day routine. Running an errand or setting personal goals only gets more fun when viewed through the lens of D&D.

That all said, there are different ways to approach adventuring in the real world. You can go it alone (don't listen to those who decry the dangers of going alone!), or you can find like-minded people to join you from time to time (it's totally okay to split the party sometimes). Your play style and adventurer type (you can learn more about those in Chapter 2) will determine *how* you go about your quests.

Solo Adventuring

You are *the hero* of your adventure—and your life. When it comes to personal growth with this style of adventuring, you take the initiative to get things done and take on quests as you see fit.

In the world of D&D, quests are often given to a PC, but in the real world, if a stranger offers a quest in your corner bar, you might want to back away slowly. Of course, you'll come across less creepy quest scenarios like babysitting or pet sitting at a moment's notice for a friend because they have to attend to an emergency or being asked to help look for the beloved comic book from your partner's childhood. These types of quests are generally part of the randomness of your daily experience, not to mention the personal quests that you're pursuing as well.

In game, character growth is often forged in dragon fire and high drama, but in your solo-adventuring life, you are free to seek out challenges that are tailored to you and that make sense based on your passions, goals, and particular skill set (learn more about tackling obstacles in your life on page 119).

You can start by identifying your strengths and weaknesses, your good and bad habits, and then look at what you want to improve and why you want to improve that attribute. Are you inspired by your PC or someone else's? Maybe you want to be more like Taako from TV on *The Adventure Zone* or Jester from *Critical Role*. Ask yourself why. What are the attributes you admire, and how can you embrace them in your day-to-day? The key to a life of adventure is a willingness to get out of your comfort zone and try new things.

So, in the game of D&D, on a player character's turn there are a few options that they can pursue. Just as a character, in the absence of an arcane focus, must have a—*checks notes*—tiny ball of bat guano and sulfur to cast *fireball*, you need to have resources to do certain things in life. In game terms, you can move or take an action, bonus action, or reaction. When you go about your day, you expend resources even if it's not monetary, like emotional or physical labor.

DM State of Mind

It's the weekend, and you're all out of plans. You want to mix things up a bit because you're in a rut or you just want to shake some of the cobwebs off and see what new adventures await. So, you go for a solo adventure. But where to start? Think of it like a Choose Your Own Adventure, except you can't peek ahead to see if you like the results.

Think through the narrative of what you're doing and how interesting it sounds. Going to the aquarium is lovely, but going to the aquarium dressed in a narwhal *kigurumi* is a recipe for smiles. Your narrative doesn't have to be that outlandish—the point of this exercise is to add something just a bit extra that might add more fun or excitement to your day at every opportunity.

You can also treat each step of the way like a series of important choices: Do you go the usual route or take a slight deviation through another neighborhood? Those little side treks can unleash new possibilities. Just don't go into your adventure with expectations of how it will turn out. Stepping even a little outside your comfort zone might work brilliantly for you one day, while others leave you feeling meh about the whole thing. Not every adventure is going to be about conquering BBEGs. Imagine how exhausting that would be! Some adventures are just about enjoying the gentle journey of learning about yourself. One of the great things about keeping a journal is at the end of the day, you can capture all the things that made it great so you have a better understanding of what types of adventures you'd like to go on in the future.

Your Adventuring Party

D&D is a game where friends in real life get together and then pretend to exist as different people who are, usually, also friends. If someone told you D&D is about fighting or magic or anything else just know one thing: they were wrong. D&D is, ultimately, about *friendship*.

Anyway, in the real world, you should be intentional about your relationships. It means doing things with purpose, being assertive instead of passive, and deliberately choosing and pursuing what's good for everyone involved in the relationship. In Chapter 7, we talked about the importance of your adventuring party, but you might be wondering right now, sure, but how is D&D going to help you create new—or maintain your current—relationships? Well, the answer is to set off on adventures together! (Or, you know, just play D&D together.)

Maybe you need a little help thinking of a fun group activity (that isn't D&D) that you can you do? Something that feels a little more adventurous? We've got you covered! Here's an activity table you can roll on to help you out. So, grab your d12 and let's have some fun!

d12	Activity
1	Avernus's Kitchen: Have a cook-off between two teams of friends.
2	Urban Explorers: Be tourists in your own city for a day.
3	Performance Check: Have an open mic night at home.
4	Idle Champions: Have a video game tournament.
5	Downtime: Enjoy a silly activity together like mini golf or balloon animal making.
6	Roleplay: LARP as your characters and go for a walk in the park.
7	Roll Dice: Have a board game weekend.
8	Fortify: Collect delivery boxes and build a backyard fort for an afternoon.
9	Bardic Inspiration: Enjoy an outdoor concert together.
10	Survival Check: Cook for each other using only ingredients that are already on hand.
11	Day of Rest: Make up a holiday, then celebrate it each year.
12	Search for Treasure: Go geocaching.

Conquering goals and having new experiences with your friends will create a lifetime of memories. Mix it up, plan your own "encounters," or make up a new table with your adventuring party, so you always have a new variety of activities to try.

Downtime

So far, you've set goals, identified hurdles, and gotten your adventuring party together for some fun times. It's great to embrace life to the fullest, but remember that it's just as important to give yourself and your party a moment to breathe. After all, life is a marathon, not a sprint—or a campaign, not a one-shot.

Okay, so maybe you've realized now that you're feeling a bit run-down and could use some time to yourself. Good news: there is something called *downtime* in D&D that is perfect to help you get some real-life R&R. Just as characters take a pause from adventuring in D&D, so too can you from your life's excitement-packed campaign, and downtime is a chance to engage in other activities and recharge your batteries. Downtime in D&D exists when PCs are between quests. This is the time to shop, rest, and have fun. Self-care is always a free action that you should allow yourself to take when you need it.

ROLL FOR SUPPORT

Rest and relaxation mean different things to different people. Roll a d6 for advice from our classic adventuring party.

1. Hank, the ranger: "Let's go camping! And by *camping*, I definitely don't mean *glamping*."
2. Eric, the fighter: "Time to hit the gym."
3. Diana, the bard: "Did someone say *party*?"
4. Presto, the wizard: "Hocus-pocus, let's read a book and focus!"
5. Sheila, the rogue: *Slips away into the night*
6. Bobby, the barbarian: "One word: skydiving."

The *Dungeon Master's Guide* lists a few downtime activities that can easily be done in real life too: crafting, practicing a profession, recuperating, researching, and training. There are other things you can do too, though you should leave pit fighting for the fantasy world. You should feel free to pursue whatever you'd like in your downtime. A lot of these activities are easy, like visiting your local park or auditing some online courses. Other downtime activities are more complex, like taking certain classes or workshops, some recreational activities, or going on a trip. Again, you know the things that will set you at ease, and if it's retail therapy, so be it—so long as it's within your means.

Even when you are taking some downtime, you can still have a little fun. Sure, the activities you do in your spare time can be related to personal growth, but ideally, you're engaging in activities to unwind or for the pleasure of it. You can also feel free to include your adventuring party in your downtime activities, but it's also perfectly fine to want to have a little time to yourself. In fact, alone time gives you the opportunity to relax and actually *rest*. Taking some alone time has also been known to help boost creativity and productivity and improve your overall happiness. Not to mention, taking space for yourself and being open to giving space to others in your party when needed are great ways to level up your relationships with friends, family members, and colleagues.

On Your Turn

Sometimes, to take care of yourself and avoid burnout, you need something more than just downtime; you need rest. Questing is fun and all, but it's also a tiring business, and there are going to be times when you just run out of spell slots. What do you do then? Well, that's easy—take a page from the *Player's Handbook* and *rest*.

In the real world, a short rest can take a few minutes, hours, or even a couple of days and can look like taking a mental health day, meditating, going for a walk, or even taking a nap. A long rest, as the name suggests, takes place over several days, weeks, or even months. This could be something like taking a vacation (or staycation), a sabbatical, or maybe taking unpaid, job-protected leave under the Family and Medical Leave Act (FMLA) if you can afford to. Just remember that every adventurer needs time to rest.

Going to do some tai chi in the park? Remember to turn off your phone or put it on vibrate so you can go with the flow distraction-free. Taking a trip? Set your out-of-office reminder, and don't look at your emails. Downtime is meant to be fairly stress-free, so take it easy if things don't go your way, or try to take a moment to redirect negative feelings into more positive ones.

You'll feel a lot better and be better prepared to return to your adventures once you're well rested.

10

An
Adventurer's
Journal

Chances are you don't travel around with a bard who is happily chronicling your day-to-day adventures or writing epic poems about the obstacles you've overcome, so you might be wondering, "How do I know that I'm *succeeding* at being more D&D?" Well, for one, you've got your actionable goals that were created in Chapter 8 (page 112). But, okay, we get it. You want to be able to see and measure your progress, right? In the world of D&D, you can gain experience points (XP) for defeating monsters, achieving goals, or just working hard at learning a new skill, and when you have enough experience, you can level up. To help you keep track of your "character progression" and all your goals, skills, and other things that you have learned on your daily adventures, one thing that might be helpful is an Adventurer's Journal.

But just writing down stats and facts about yourself isn't going to be much help to you in the long run (plus it would make for a pretty boring tale around the fire), so you might want to think about journaling as you go about your daily adventures. Why? Well, when you take time to reflect, you have an opportunity to look back on an event or a moment from a place of experience—because you already lived it—and learn from mistakes, be grateful, and get a better understanding of yourself.

There are also some skills and traits that tend to develop over time and that you can start to specialize in once you begin to recognize patterns in interests, activities, or other things in your journal. For example, you might notice that for the last month you've been ordering from a certain restaurant or have been more adventurous with the different foods you eat, so maybe it is time to develop your culinary skills and try a cooking class to level them up. Or maybe you have been regularly pet sitting for your friend for the last year and you've realized that you enjoy spending time with animals and want to raise your Animal Handling skills by volunteering at your local animal shelter. Using a journal can also help you track certain milestones during your quests so that you can see how you're progressing on your quest to meditate more by allowing you to check off every week that you meditated three days out of the week. Here's 10 XP, coming at you!

However, if a regular paper or digital journal seems like too much work, don't fret because there are many apps available that can help gamify parts of your life like *Habitica*, which rewards you, as the name suggests, for building good habits, or *Zombies, Run!*, which encourages exercise by helping you pretend undead hordes are chasing you—let's hope they're slow zombies! There are also unique traditional journal options like the Hero's Journal for helping to journal your goals. You can also copy the following information into your favorite journal for more room to write and continue your journey of self-discovery.

Just remember, regardless of how you want to keep track of your progress, applying elements of D&D to your life should be fun, so *you* decide how much or how little you want to do regarding any of the above.

Character Sheet

A character sheet is an iconic and essential part of the D&D experience. Throughout this book, there are activities and opportunities for you to create and explore your own real-life "character" by using this character sheet below. Feel free to refer back to the previous chapters to help you fill out and answer the following sections.

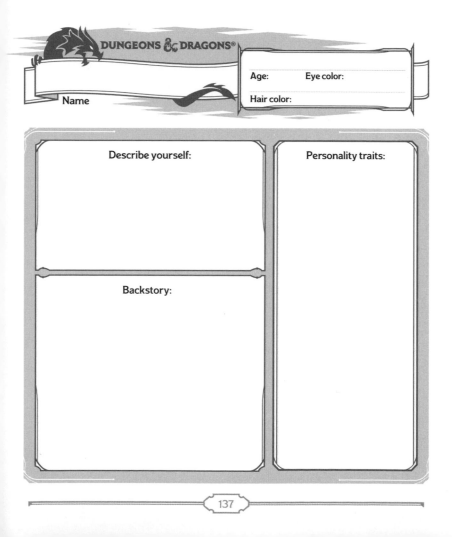

DUNGEONS & DRAGONS®

Name

Age:　　　Eye color:

Hair color:

Describe yourself:

Personality traits:

Backstory:

Level:

Next milestone:

Experience point goal:

STRENGTH

DEXTERITY

CONSTITUTION

INTELLIGENCE

WISDOM

CHARISMA

List two or three ideals:

List two or three bonds:

List two or three flaws:

Communication style:

Support languages:

Primary adventurer type:

Secondary adventurer type:

Who are your allies?

_____
_____
_____
_____

What is something that you treasure most?

_____
_____

Who would be in your adventuring party and why?

_____
_____
_____
_____
_____
_____
_____
_____
_____
_____
_____
_____
_____

List 3 of your strengths:

_____
_____
_____

List 3 things that you want to overcome:

_____
_____
_____

What is one "dungeon" or "dragon" that you recently overcame?

_____
_____
_____
_____
_____
_____
_____
_____

List 4 things that inspire you:

_____
_____
_____
_____

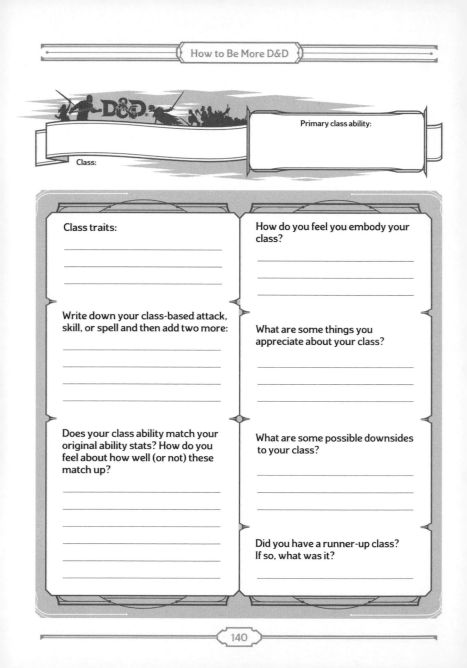

Primary class ability:

Class:

Class traits:

_____
_____
_____

Write down your class-based attack, skill, or spell and then add two more:

_____
_____
_____
_____

Does your class ability match your original ability stats? How do you feel about how well (or not) these match up?

_____
_____
_____
_____
_____

How do you feel you embody your class?

_____
_____
_____

What are some things you appreciate about your class?

_____
_____
_____

What are some possible downsides to your class?

_____
_____
_____

Did you have a runner-up class? If so, what was it?

_____

Dungeon Master role:

_____

List four skills that you think are important for a DM to have.

_____

_____

_____

_____

Which DM role do you feel most drawn to? Which DM role do you feel the least confident about? Why?

_____

_____

_____

_____

_____

_____

Write about a situation, problem, or event when you wished you could've had a DM there to help you see the bigger picture. If you were the DM guiding a player through this scenario, what would you have done or said to help them?

_____

_____

_____

_____

_____

_____

_____

_____

_____

_____

_____

_____

_____

_____

Encounter Log

When dealing with life's challenges, wouldn't it be nice to know what you're up against? In Chapter 2, we explored how you can turn everyday tasks and obstacles into "encounters." Then later in Chapter 8, we talked about looking at how personal goals, projects, or problems can be treated as encounters as well. From saving that baby skunk that's hiding under your porch to your uneasiness giving presentations, there are a variety of different challenges or obstacles to tackle here. First, you can name the encounter (because sometimes things seem more manageable when you put a name to them) and then write out the objective or end goal, then any obstacles you might face and any party members (or people who are there to help support you). Next, you can start to figure out how to overcome the problem at hand.

And if you want to gamify things a bit, you can even assign a reward or XP to each challenge in your Encounter Log. In D&D, each monster has an XP value, but, for the sake of simplicity, in real life you can use certain personal milestones or a predetermined number to work toward for leveling up if you want. For example, you start off at level 1 and can level up after you pay off a certain amount on your credit card. Then you set your next milestone goal. Different individuals find different things challenging, so your Difficulty Class (or level) for each obstacle in your manual will likely look very different from someone else's. While the vast majority of people have a fear of public speaking and would assign it about 10 stars, an extroverted theater geek may find it a breeze and rank it as a 1- or 2-star challenge.

If you receive a little help along the way, don't forget to share the wealth. You can celebrate by showing your gratitude, with a simple thank-you or a nice gesture for smaller encounters or a gift or special treat to show your appreciation for bigger ones.

Reaching Your Goals

When it comes to accomplishing your goals and leveling up, in D&D there are two ways to approach it: XP or milestones. This is where you can decide just how deeply you want to delve in terms of gamifying your life. With XP, you keep track of experience points before leveling, which means you need to outline how many points you need to reach the next tier, whereas milestones look at important events or moments in your life that help you to grow or get closer to a goal.

Here is an example that uses XP: Drink water three glasses of water a day (5 XP). Then each day you complete this goal you get to add 5 XP to your total. When you reach your goal XP, you get to level up! This could easily be changed into a milestone if that is what you are tracking at the time. For more complex goals, you can write out "Potential Challenges" and assign a Difficulty Class (see page 142) to the possible problems and XP to the possible solutions. "Actions" are the things you planned out to meet your goal. For more help building and tracking your goals, turn back to Chapter 8, page 117.

ENCOUNTER LOG

Quest	Actions	XP Tracker
Goal:	1.	Date:
	2.	
	3.	
	4.	
Target Date:	5.	
Side Quests (Subgoals)	Potential Challenges	Progress:
1.	Problems:	
2.		
3.		
Cost (Monetary/Time)		
	Solutions:	

As you can see, there are a lot of ways to gamify your experiences or approach journaling in a way that's inspired by D&D. The character sheet and encounter log on the previous pages are our tools to help you get started on your journey, but don't hesitate to take these examples and run with them. Use them to help you reflect on changes you want to make or modify them to better fit your life and goals. Just remember: Have fun on your life's adventure.

Conclusion

The World Is Your Adventure

Congratulations! You have come a long way on your journey! Hopefully this book has helped you feel more equipped to bring a sense of adventure, balance, and D&D flair into your everyday life. Don't forget, there are plenty of ways—both big and small—to embrace D&D in the real world, and the topics covered in this book only scratch the surface. Feel free to take what works for you and build on it, and if you are ever stuck, then, hey, that is what the d20 is for, right?

As for me and my journey? Well, I wound up packing up my entire life on the east coast of Canada, selling a house and most of my belongings, to eventually move to the Pacific Northwest in the USA. We got married and had a kid, and I changed careers from freelance writer to game designer. And, yeah, I write for D&D and 5E products now, among other things.

The geeky child in me who used to code text adventure games would be pretty proud. Heck, the broken adult I was before starting on this path is for sure. To think my life could have gone a totally different route if I'd not been open to the opportunities—if I hadn't taken calculated risks. I never would have imagined an RPG could be such a huge catalyst for change in my life. While it doesn't need to have the same impact on you, this game and the many things you can learn from it can leave a lasting impression away from the game table.

My hope for you is that the information in this book helped you find inspiration to feel more confident, push your boundaries, tackle those obstacles, strengthen your relationships, and maybe look at D&D in a new way. Of course, not everything in life is going to be a critical hit. But sometimes when the die rolls a 1, remember that doesn't mean you've failed, but maybe it's time to take a step back, get in touch with yourself and those around you, and just roll with it!

ACKNOWLEDGMENTS

Dungeons & Dragons has been such a positive force of change and good in my life, so to be able to write a book about using the principles of the game in real life has been an incredible experience that I could not have dreamed of on my own. There are so many people in my life who have been a part of my journey, but this book would not exist without my brilliant editor, Britny Brooks-Perilli. When she approached me with the concept, I could not have said yes any faster. With her guidance, kindness, and incredible insight, this book was able to come to life. Of course, there's one person who introduced me to the game itself and then the wider world of TTRPGs, and that is my partner, Chris Tulach. He encourages me to be the brave adventurer that I've become, and I'm so grateful for the life we have built together. Thanks also to Wizards of the Coast for having faith in me to pull this off with the right tone and knowledge base to make this a fun and informative book. I've also had many D&D groups over the course of the years made up of family, friends, and strangers at conventions or game shops. Many thanks to my Saturday Sellswords group: Jason Megatron Burrows, Kelly Knox, Kage Freudigmann, and Bianca Bickford. And thanks to the sometimes rotating cast of players in my Sunday game, who helped a fledgling player explore the game in such an entertaining and safe space. Finally, a huge shout-out to the d20 Dames and the community we've built together. Jen Vaughn, Brittni Leigh Liyanage,

ACKNOWLEDGMENTS

Meris Mullaley, and Jessica Ross are my Sistren Pentagram. May we support, love, and fight for one another into old age.

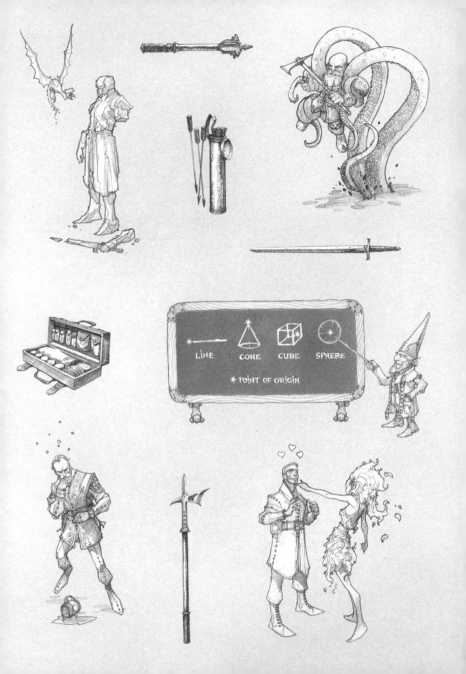

LINE · CONE · CUBE · SPHERE

✴ POINT OF ORIGIN